More praise for *Transformative HR*

"With its focus on the power of evidence-based change, *Transformative HR* takes the practice of effective talent management to a new arena. The principles it presents incorporate the best of HR fundamentals and offer a new level of sophistication for today's human capital leaders. Backed by real-world examples and written by two of the most respected thinkers in HR today, *Transformative HR* is a must-read for HR leaders."

—Edward E. Lawler III, director, Center for Effective Organizations and Distinguished Professor of Business, University of Southern California; author, *Management Reset: Organizing for Sustainable Effectiveness*

"This book highlights a critical area for successful HR professionals and business leaders, bringing science and rigor to the decisions that organizations make about talent. At the end of the day we all have to make choices, and Boudreau and Jesuthasan provide us with the road map for ensuring that those choices deliver the greatest value to our organizations."

—Stephen J. Cerrone, PhD, executive vice president, human resources, Sara Lee Corp.

Transformative HR

How Great Companies Use Evidence-Based Change for Sustainable Advantage

John W. Boudreau

and

Ravin Jesuthasan

with Towers Watson
with valuable assistance from David Creelman

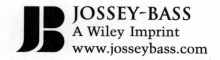

JOSSEY-BASS
A Wiley Imprint
www.josseybass.com

Published by Jossey-Bass
A Wiley Imprint
989 Market Street, San Francisco, CA 94103-1741—www.josseybass.com

Readers should be aware that Internet Web sites offered as citations and/or sources for further information may have changed or disappeared between the time this was written and when it is read.

Limit of Liability/Disclaimer of Warranty: While the publisher and author have used their best efforts in preparing this book, they make no representations or warranties with respect to the accuracy or completeness of the contents of this book and specifically disclaim any implied warranties of merchantability or fitness for a particular purpose. No warranty may be created or extended by sales representatives or written sales materials. The advice and strategies contained herein may not be suitable for your situation. You should consult with a professional where appropriate. Neither the publisher nor author shall be liable for any loss of profit or any other commercial damages, including but not limited to special, incidental, consequential, or other damages.

Jossey-Bass books and products are available through most bookstores. To contact Jossey-Bass directly call our Customer Care Department within the U.S. at 800-956-7739, outside the U.S. at 317-572-3986, or fax 317-572-4002.

Wiley also publishes its books in a variety of electronic formats and by print-on-demand. Some material included with standard print versions of this book may not be included in e-books or in print-on-demand. If the version of this book that you purchased references media such as CD or DVD that was not included in your purchase, you may download this material at http://booksupport.wiley.com. For more information about Wiley products, visit www.wiley.com.

Library of Congress Cataloging-in-Publication Data

Boudreau, John W.
   Transformative HR: how great companies use evidence-based change for sustainable advantage / John W. Boudreau and Ravin Jesuthasan with Towers Watson. — 1
      p. cm.
   Includes index.
   ISBN 978-1-118-03604-4 (hardback), ISBN 978-1-118-10249-7 (ebk),
   ISBN 978-1-118-10250-3 (ebk), ISBN 978-1-118-10251-0 (ebk)
   1. Personnel management.   2. Leadership.   3. Organizational change.   I. Jesuthasan,
Ravin, 1968–   II. Towers, Watson.   III. Title.
   HF5549.B77265 2011
   658.3—dc23

                                                                                    2011021817

Printed in Singapore
FIRST EDITION
HB Printing 10 9 8 7 6 5 4 3 2 1

Contents

To my family and colleagues, who inspire me every day
with their random acts of generosity
—John Boudreau

To my parents, Daniel and Karuna, who invested so much in me; to
my wife, Maureen, whose encouragement and support
made this book possible; to my children, Nadia and Daniel,
who inspire me every day
— Ravin Jesuthasan

Acknowledgments

This book is the result of tireless dedication on the part of an amazing team of people at Towers Watson. Our project managers—Nell Stanton, Andrea Cure, and Kate Walania—were pivotal to ensuring that we completed this book; they endured more trauma in seven months than anyone should have to suffer in a lifetime.

We thank the editorial staff, particularly Anne McKneally, who reviewed and read every chapter countless times, and Sharon Congdon, who caught many typos.

We also thank the marketing department, particularly Corrinne Macias, Graham Spencer, and Nancy Connors, for their support through every phase of this project.

Thanks as well to the Towers Watson consultants who invested countless hours in helping us tell the stories of the great companies in this book: Angel Hoover, Michael Drawhorn, Sylvia Branke, Julie Darst, Mark Flavin, David Eisenreich, Lori Swope, Elise Schroeter, Emmett Seaborn, Samira Kaderali, Stephen Young, and Eric Chai.

We are also grateful for the sponsorship and support of Julie Gebauer, Managing Director of Towers Watson's Talent and Rewards segment.

We wish to thank the executives at each of our case study companies for sharing their stories with us. Specifically, we would like to acknowledge the efforts of the following people with whom we worked over the course of many months, and who helped make their companies' participation possible: Penny Meier and Kelli Hunter of Ameriprise; Hilda Piell and Francie

Sisul of CME Group; Ed Stephenson and Terry Hildebrand of Coca-Cola; Torsten Bittlingmaier of Deutsche Telekom; Shahnaz Al-Sadat Abdul Mohsein and Kamal Nawawi of Khazanah Nasional; Bei Ling and Joan Gulley of PNC Bank; Per Scott of the Royal Bank of Canada; Greig Aitken of the Royal Bank of Scotland; and Jean Zhang of Shanda Interactive Entertainment, Ltd.

In addition, we wish to acknowledge our editor at Jossey-Bass, Kathe Sweeney, for being such a pleasure to work with and for making this experience far easier than it should have been.

Introduction

The Promise of Evidence-Based Change

Evidence-based change is a mind-set and approach to making HR decisions. In evidence-based change, the principles covered in the first five chapters of this book are combined with a robust change-management process to ensure a sustainable competitive advantage for the organization.

The thinking behind evidence-based change was inspired in part by the evidence-based movement in medicine. That movement came about after medical researchers noticed that doctors, despite a vast amount of available medical research, were treating disease in idiosyncratic ways. They were using their own preferred treatments even when there was solid scientific evidence that other treatments were more effective. The evidence-based medicine movement encouraged doctors to determine, on the basis of the available evidence, which treatment for a particular disease was most effective and to apply that treatment. (This was hardly a radical notion, but human nature is such that people, even doctors, sometimes need a push to behave with scientific rationality.)

In matters of people management, too, decisions are often made without full reliance on evidence. In recruiting, for example, there is evidence that unstructured interviews are far less effective than more structured approaches in identifying the best candidates, and yet despite the evidence unstructured interviews are still the preferred method of many managers. Organizations with a strong and well-informed HR function often now take a more structured approach to interviewing—a victory for an evidence-based approach to HR. The HR profession can also claim to have taken a step forward and become more evidence-based in its use of scientifically designed employee surveys and scientifically designed goal setting in performance management.

These are the exceptions, however, not the norm. More often than not, decisions about HR and people management are made on the basis of the instincts or uninformed preferences of stakeholders. The future of the HR profession lies in improving its ability to make decisions based on evidence. That evidence may be from research studies, as was the case with structured interviews, but more commonly it is based on a clearly articulated logic informed by both qualitative and quantitative data. HR will never have the precision of engineering, but as we will see in this book, many organizations have gone a long way toward bringing a great deal of rigor to HR decision making.

Evidence-Based Change Principles in Action: Drawing the Right Conclusions

Imagine for a moment that you lead the human resources function of a major urban hospital, with more than five thousand employees. When organizational leaders' annual performance scores come in, two profiles jump out at you:

Leader 1: Very high customer-satisfaction levels, low employee turnover, very high employee-engagement scores

Leader 2: Rock-bottom customer-satisfaction levels, high employee turnover, employee-engagement scores only slightly above average

Which of these two people would you expect to be the better leader? Whom do you think needs additional training? Who might even be facing termination if things don't improve?

Let's also assume that you are experiencing extraordinary pressure to play a significant role in boosting your hospital's competitiveness in its region, both as an employer of choice and as a provider of patient-centric services, so that the community will come to your hospital instead of going to the one down the block. This means that you have to prune your people in such a way that employees as well as patients are happy. Again, whom would you keep? Whom would you let go?

The choice seems obvious and immediate. Leader 1 has happy customers and very low turnover. Employee engagement is high under this leader. This individual is stellar on all three performance metrics. Leader 2, by contrast, has low scores on employee engagement. Why are so many people leaving this leader's unit? And if the customers aren't happy either, what could possibly be the rationale for retaining this person? It would seem that this leader is meeting neither the goal of boosting the hospital's competitiveness nor the goal of making the hospital an employer of choice.

So what will you do? Keep leader 1 and lose leader 2? In light of the performance indices alone, that would be the obvious decision. In light of the organizational objectives, however, it would most likely be the wrong decision.

Let's look more closely at who these two people are, and at what they mean to your hospital and to the community overall.

Leader 1 is the head of a cardiovascular unit. His team is tightly knit, highly skilled, and collegial. And the hours are reasonable (8 AM to 4:30 PM), allowing for a balanced life that syncs with the schedules of family members and friends—a rare experience for people who work in health care. The patients are profoundly satisfied with the results of this unit's work because they can see immediate and obvious improvements in their quality of life. This leader is enjoying the trifecta of a successful performance record at the hospital—grateful customers, happy employees, and talent that stays.

Leader 2, by contrast, is the head of the hospital's food service division. Patient-satisfaction scores are predictably low (hospital food is conventionally unpopular). The employee population includes a significant number of people who don't speak English, the language in which the engagement survey is produced. Many of the moderately satisfied workers chose to ignore the survey, with the result that this leader's employee-satisfaction scores are misleadingly low. The reason his department is experiencing such high turnover is not that his people are unhappy with their boss. In fact, he has created an extended family with his people, who hold him up as a beloved patriarch. The high turnover stems instead from the fact that he hires entry-level employees and teaches them essential work habits and life skills that equip them for better jobs, either within the hospital or out in the community, so many of them leave to take good jobs elsewhere or are promoted.

At first glance, it would be understandable if the dilemma represented by this scenario were seen simply as an example of what happens when HR and the departments it supports rely too much on any form of data, without taking the time to fully understand what that information means on a multilevel, organizational scale. Metrics run amok. But if senior leaders in HR don't stop to fully consider the reality behind the performance scores for the heads of these two units, then senior HR leaders can easily make the mistake of trying to fix the wrong thing, imposing inappropriate values or objectives on one or another of these unit heads. They might even cause that person to become disengaged and, by extension, produce the same reaction in hundreds of potentially valuable workers. That could easily be the outcome if HR and the leaders it serves were to use performance data strictly in measure-and-response mode, which is the way data are too often used in HR organizations today.

So, evidence-based change is not simply creating data and acting on it. In this book, we invite you to consider how evidence-based change defines the next generation of HR within a much broader context that incorporates logic, strategic awareness, and savvy change management. The phrase *evidence-based change* refers to transforming organizations on the basis of well-grounded evidence and skillful influence and change management, rather than gut feelings, knee-jerk responses, or copying competitors' practices. This approach extends the collection and analysis of data (such as performance) by using five important principles that elevate the data and their analysis to a new level, one that transforms organizations to create true strategic impact. When HR approaches its role with these five principles in mind, the collection and analysis of data produce insights and solutions that are far more nuanced and optimized to the organization's context and systems, and thus more likely to create change that is more richly impactful and sustainable.

The Five Principles of Evidence-Based Change

Our example of the hospital is based on a true story and illustrates how HR leaders can ask better questions, find better answers, and run vastly more dynamic and business-relevant HR operations for their corporations. They can achieve these outcomes by using a disciplined approach to what might initially be perceived as merely thorny or "intuitive" talent-management issues. In other words, leading-edge HR functions are helping their organizations achieve greater success and create a more fulfilling work environment for their people by relying on five principles of evidence-based change:

1. Logic-driven analytics
2. Segmentation
3. Risk leverage
4. Integration and synergy
5. Optimization

Logic-Driven Analytics

To return to the hospital where you serve as HR leader, let's say you think at first that you are being analytical, and therefore a "smart" partner to your senior leadership team, by handily serving up three measurements to gauge leadership acumen. Indeed, most leaders outside HR welcome, even demand, that HR issues be boiled down to a small set of consistent measures like these. But you quickly see that it is much too simplistic to expect one set of metrics to apply to all the leaders of this very complex organization, with its many constituencies and its wide variety of employee populations, ranging from entry-level food service workers to neurosurgeons. You understand that one set clearly does not fit all, and that there are nuances that, if observed, can lead you to much more robust conclusions and understandings of how your hospital can truly function at its optimum.

In fact, it is HR's role not only to be aware of these vital nuances but also to approach HR's systems, measures, and relationships with key constituents in such a way that the nuances are recognized, and organizational leaders are held accountable to a higher level of sophistication in analysis and decision making. This higher level is characterized by what we call *logic-driven analytics*.

An example of using logic-driven analytics would be recognizing why survey scores that would suggest poor performance in the cardiovascular world might actually indicate excellent leadership of a team of food service workers in their first jobs. The logic rests on the fact that part of the organization's objective in the food service area is to develop relatively early-stage talent so that those employees can be ready for deployment throughout the hospital, having been trained in a work ethic specifically suited to the organization. Thus, success requires hiring those who may be less emotionally connected to the work, those who are more likely to be promoted or move on to better jobs in other organizations, and those who must deal with the reality of hospital food quality. This is very different from the cardiovascular unit, which draws a population already deeply qualified and committed to the work, stable in their career, and creating life-saving changes in patient lives. The appropriate goal for human capital standards, investments, and developmental approaches in the food service division is to yield a cadre of well-trained employees who can then move within or outside the organization, whereas the appropriate goal for the cardiovascular unit is to take seasoned professionals and create a world-class team.

Segmentation

Logic-driven analytics often produces insights like this, showing that one unit or employee group is very different from another. This leads to the principle of *segmentation*. In the hospital example the entire analysis rested on recognizing food services and cardiology as distinct segments that may need to be treated differently. It is a straightforward idea, but one that conflicts with a long-held HR tradition of resisting any attempt to give one group "special treatment." Yet applying different standards about what counts as a good engagement score for a cardiology leader and a food services leader doesn't impinge on fairness. Indeed, using logic-based analysis to identify and understand differences can actually increase fairness.

While segmentation is one of the most common tools used in evidence-based change, it is possible to go overboard. HR must understand where segmentation is vital to the organization and where it is less necessary. A standard set of leadership measures may be adequate for 80 percent of the organization's leaders but disastrous for the other 20 percent. Therefore, the next generation of HR must acknowledge these differences, communicate them, and then motivate actions that reflect them as well as the consequent need to divide the workforce into segments for the purpose of evaluation.

Returning once again to our hospital example, let's say that in order to get the most out of your organization's developmental and leadership investments in its food service unit, you start thinking of this function as a sort of farm team for the rest of your hospital. Once you have identified the vital importance of distinguishing between the food service segment and the cardiovascular segment, you see different ways to invest in each of them. The entire employment proposition and life cycle will be different for each segment, not only because the employee populations have distinct needs and backgrounds but also because the two units serve such different roles in the talent pipeline. Making those investments properly is the principle of optimization, discussed later, but optimization almost always requires segmentation, which involves understanding differences and their importance.

Risk Leverage

Next-generation HR is not simply about reducing the risk of turnover or low performance. It is also about the practice of *risk leverage*. In other words, it is about knowing when—and when not—to take risks.

For example, from a simplistic perspective, the high level of turnover in food service would be defined as a higher risk in the area of talent, and it would be a reason for holding the leader accountable for reducing that risk. But evidence-based change requires that risk in the food service unit be seen as different from risk in the cardiovascular unit. Yes, turnover in the food service unit is a risk, but it is far less significant than the risk of promoting employees who will fail later on because the food service unit didn't sufficiently develop their basic employment habits or vet them for future employability. The latter risk affects how well the unit produces employees able to grow within the organization, serving its many needs for decades. Some of those people may initially present themselves as diamonds in the rough, and so if the leader of your food service unit is pressed too hard to reduce the risk of turnover, that leader may not groom individuals for future positions, for fear employees will leave for better jobs elsewhere. The right level of risk requires taking some risk of employees leaving for other employers, in order to get the value of the grooming that occurs for future jobs at the hospital.

By concentrating fundamental developmental tasks in a function such as food service, HR also manages another aspect of workforce risk—the risk of error or noncompliant behavior. Food safety is a critical concern in the hospital, of course, but a hospital is not a five-star restaurant. So, some food quality variation is an acceptable risk, when it gives the organization a place where those with rudimentary employment skills can be employed and groomed. By concentrating elementary developmental phases in food service and setting standards in food service that are different from those of the cardiovascular unit, HR optimizes risk.

Integration and Synergy

Recognizing the differences in needs and risk among vital workforce segments is a start, but it is also important that things work well together. This is the principle of *integration and synergy*. This can happen at many levels. It includes how the individual HR practices work together, but it also includes how the HR processes in different units work together across the organization. When the principle of integration and synergy is in play, combinations add up to more than the sum of their parts: $1 + 1 = 3$.

In the hospital, for instance, the food service unit must actually work in synergy with talent needs in the rest of the hospital. If food service is merely regarded as a closed system designed to achieve an appropriate standard of food service performance, then typical practice will be to hire to those standards, reward employees for food service outcomes, and weed out workers solely on the basis of job performance. Synergy, however, suggests that the food service unit serves a larger purpose—its employees are regarded as a farm team for other positions elsewhere in the hospital. Therefore, the leader of the food service unit, much more than the leader of the cardiovascular unit, must combine HR practices to create not only great performance but also great potential. At the level of HR practices, synergy means the combination of (1) a performance incentive that rewards patient-centric service both within and outside the core job and (2) a hiring standard that looks for a strong service orientation, not just food-preparation ability, and offers an opportunity to produce food service workers with the passion to excel elsewhere in the organization. Combining training in such topics as food service and food safety/handling skills with training in teamwork produces better-trained food service workers as well as workers who have been vetted and prepared for future talent demands throughout the hospital.

Optimization

Optimization means making the right investments, investing more where it will make a big difference, and having the courage to make smaller investments where the difference is less. It means knowing the right balance between standardizing and customizing. The insights from principles like segmentation, risk leverage, integration and synergy, and logic-driven analytics often lead to the uncomfortable conclusion that getting it right means doing things differently in different places.

In the hospital, turnover in the food service unit is regretted, but probably not as significantly as turnover among cardiovascular professionals. The hospital might optimize by investing in retention reduction strategies like high pay and tenure-based benefits *less* in the food service unit than in the cardiovascular unit. On the contrary, the hospital might invest more in mentoring for food service workers than in its cardiovascular unit. An investment in mentoring better fits the goal of taking people with raw potential and turning them into valuable long-term employees. Optimization is all about redirecting investments away from areas with low impact to areas of higher value based on the evidence.

Optimization questions some assumptions like "hire the best person for each role." In the hospital, high selection standards are absolutely appropriate in the cardiovascular unit, where you don't want people learning basic work skills and habits on the job; you want them ready from day one. But if you apply the same selection standard to the food service unit, you not only will delay fulfilling your immediate needs for staff but also will rob yourself of the opportunity to recruit candidates that may be "rough," where you can serve the role of preparing them for the hospital's more general talent pipeline.

Optimization is all about acting on the evidence even when it means redirecting investments from well-liked but low-impact programs toward higher-impact programs, and doing so even when it means treating different groups differently.

Mental Models for HR Decisions

An evidence-based approach to HR serves a dual purpose—it helps HR leaders make the right decisions about people, and it helps those HR leaders engage other organizational stakeholders in a decision process that collaboratively reaches the right decisions.

In the absence of an evidence-based approach, however, the organization's non-HR managers typically apply certain familiar mental models to HR situations. To understand motivation, for example, managers draw their insights not from psychology, the science of human behavior, but instead from the more familiar framework of economics. Economics-based models make the assumption that humans are perfectly rational and driven entirely by incentives. Although such assumptions are erroneous, most economists feel that these assumptions work well enough for economic purposes. But organizational managers steeped in economic thinking may apply such models too directly. For example, research shows that social justice and group loyalty may constitute very

(*Continued*)

strong motivations for employees, but there is evidence of managers assuming that employees are motivated purely by self-interest and are likely to try to take every advantage.

Accounting provides another set of mental models in which organizational managers are steeped. Accounting models often position people as a cost. Therefore, organizational managers steeped in accounting models are driven to cut headcounts and to reduce expenses for compensation and training. In a manufacturing environment, of course, managers see machinery as an element of production; they don't suggest replacing high-quality machines with inferior equipment just to save money. Managers in nonmanufacturing environments need frameworks that will help them think about investments in human resources with the same rigor that is brought to bear on manufacturing-sector decisions about investments in machinery.

HR could develop its own mental models as the foundation for an evidence-based approach, but there is good reason to look to outside models, especially models with which organizational managers are already comfortable. One such model is that of consumer behavior. Managers know that consumers are influenced by trust in brands, by loyalty, by social factors, and by a host of other irrational elements. After all, Christian Dior does not package its perfume in cheap plastic bottles and claim that consumers make choices solely on the basis of economic factors. By using familiar mental models like this one, HR can get organizational managers to jettison simplistic or otherwise unhelpful models and think more clearly about motivating people.

Evidence-Based Change: The Promise

Let's return one more time to our example of the hospital and to your imaginary role as the leader of its HR function. As your new approach to measuring and assessing leadership gains traction throughout the organization, members of your leadership community (and most likely their direct reports as well) begin to notice that leaders are managing and motivating their employees in ways that are appropriate to each function—ideally, they are getting the best performance out of each group. Food service leaders who reduce turnover by making few demands on their people are quickly revealed and corrected. Food service leaders who set rigorous and specific expectations to build skill sets that prepare their employees for their future are encouraged and supported—even celebrated—for their high promotion rates. Cardiovascular leaders, on the other hand, are celebrated for their ability to create loyalty, commitment, and low turnover among a rare and highly qualified group of professionals.

When gut feelings no longer drive strategy, you and your leaders make better decisions. For example, if you think the food service leader is undervalued when held up to the standard measures, in part because he is overseeing the hospital's farm team, then transformative HR means articulating your case and developing propositions that will allow it to be tested as you gather evidence to engage the debate. Questions like these drive an evidence-based approach:

How many employees get promoted out of food service, by comparison with promotions out of other units?

How much variation in employee-engagement scores can be attributed not to the food service leader but to the expectations of his unit's "customers"?

How often do hiring managers in other areas of the hospital, or in the community at large, draw candidates from the food service unit because they know about the high caliber of those workers?

Although you may know intuitively that your future talent pool is being groomed in food service, that knowledge is a hard sell if you have to present your case to organizational leaders accustomed to applying rigorous business disciplines to other aspects of the business. But when you use logic-driven analytics to formulate and then support your point of view, you may very well discover that your instinctual perceptions are soundly supported, and even amplified, by your experiences and by the observations you have made with the use of business analytics.

Perhaps more important, when HR leaders translate their intuitive knowledge into propositions that can be tested, they invite their constituents to join them as true colleagues. But if HR is seen as involving something that can't be measured, something that can be experienced intuitively only by a few talented people, then there is little incentive for organizational leaders, employees, and other stakeholders outside HR to engage with objective questions. Instead, the approach is just to hire an HR professional with a good "gut."

Traditionally, HR simply delivered the data requested by organizational leaders, with little attempt to help synthesize the information, place it into usable contexts, or explain the nuances behind it.

The next phase of development brought HR professionals into the general organizational conversation, where they helped leaders parse the data according to the questions these leaders had originally posed, and where they also helped leaders take the initial steps in applying logic to their decisions.

Now, with HR having matured and gained stature in organizations, HR leaders have grown increasingly accustomed to making rigorous human capital decisions on the basis of metrics and analytics.

Transformative HR means going even further and truly embedding analytical discipline and sophisticated systems thinking into the organization's DNA in order to create the kinds of understanding that drive better strategies and better workplace outcomes. The new iteration of HR, which we see emerging in our work with leading organizations, reflects the five principles of evidence-based change and puts HR where companies need it to be—creating superior organizational strategic success through synergistic human capital decisions and investments that span the employment life cycle and organizational design decisions.

Perhaps it is helpful to contrast the typical state of HR today with what we hope will become commonplace in the future. The following table summarizes four basic differences between HR now and HR in a future where evidence-based HR is the norm.

EVIDENCE-BASED CHANGE	
Typical HR Today	*Transformative HR Future*
• Evidence of HR value-added is rare	• Evidence of HR value is routinely provided
• HR data and analysis do not engage action	• HR data and analysis motivate strategically vital actions
• HR constituents do not routinely use HR evidence in change efforts	• HR constituents routinely demand and use HR evidence to direct strategic change
• HR is valued for its perspective on functional processes and outcomes	• HR is valued for its unique perspective on how to achieve strategic success

Similarly, application of each of the five principles will lead to a transformed HR quite different from the world of today. These differences are summarized in the following table.

LOGIC-DRIVEN ANALYTICS	
Typical HR Today	*Transformative HR Future*
• Information overload	• Information optimization
• Data reflect IT system priorities	• Data reflect HR's needs for decision making
• Lots of numbers, but no "story"	• Data and analysis focused on the vital issues
• Analysis fails to engage constituents	• Analysis is that demanded by key constituents
• Logic models for HR issues are ad hoc	• Logic models for HR issues are common and widely understood

(Continued)

SEGMENTATION

Typical HR Today	Transformative HR Future
• Organization reluctant to treat different segments differently	• Organization naturally treats different segments differently where it makes sense
• Employment customization versus standardization decisions are ad hoc	• Employment customization versus standardization decisions based on common logical frameworks
• How strategic value of different employee groups varies is poorly understood	• How strategic value of different employee groups varies is routinely analyzed and reported
• "More is better" is assumed for performance, engagement, and so on	• "Return on improved performance" is routinely considered for investments in performance, engagement, and so on

RISK LEVERAGE

Typical HR Today	Transformative HR Future
• HR risk rarely receives attention	• HR risk is routinely analyzed and considered
• Risk reduction	• Risk optimization
• HR risk is ill-defined	• HR risk elements are well understood
• HR risk analysis is ad hoc	• HR risk analysis follows common logical rules

INTEGRATION AND SYNERGY

Typical HR Today	Transformative HR Future
• Individual HR processes operate in silos	• HR processes operate as interconnected systems
• HR programs implemented and evaluated independently	• HR programs implemented and evaluated for greatest combined effect ("1 + 1 = 3")
• HR priorities established separately in different organizational units	• HR priorities established jointly across multiple organizational units
• HR systems focus on unit-specific performance goals	• HR systems focus on trade-offs that optimize performance across organizational units

OPTIMIZATION

Typical HR Today	Transformative HR Future
• Fairness is seen as equal treatment or "peanut butter" approach with investments spread equally across all groups	• Fairness is understood to mean strategically differentiated treatment
• Focus is on justifying investments in HR	• Focus is on HR investments with the largest strategic impact
• HR programs rarely canceled even as new programs are added	• HR investments routinely reduced in some areas and redeployed elsewhere

The lesson of this book is that the transformative future is not an idle dream; many organizations have made great strides toward applying the principles of evidence-based change and reaping the rewards. The chapters that follow explain these ideas in more detail and, just as important, provide many real cases that show how they can be applied.

Transformative HR

Part One

THE FIVE PRINCIPLES OF EVIDENCE-BASED CHANGE

1

INFORMATION OVERLOAD OR PERSUASIVE ANALYTICS?

Logic-driven analytics, the first principle of evidence-based change, is about identifying the most pivotal issues that an organization needs to focus on and then using robust analysis to describe those issues as well as the likely outcomes from addressing them. The use of logic-driven analytics also ensures commonality in the frameworks and mental models used in analyzing issues and defining success.

Not long ago, it was widely agreed that a lack of metrics hindered the HR profession's ability to demonstrate its value, influence key decision makers, and uncover insights into the effects of human capital on strategic success. Today—according to Boudreau and Ramstad (2007), and as observed by Cascio and Boudreau (2010)—the hard work of the HR profession, and of the thought leaders on HR measurement, has led to an embarrassment of riches. Information overload is now far more prevalent than the lack of data. Just consider the extensive numbers produced by the typical HR information system. It is often possible to generate statistics—such as turnover rates, salary costs, demographic distributions, competency inventories, and employee-opinion levels—at the touch of a key, and to "cut" those statistics to focus in on business units, individual leaders, and specific employee groups, product lines, or regions.

This is not to say that the data HR wants are always just sitting in the HR information system, waiting to be used. Many

HR and business leaders find that the available information is often not suited to their strategic questions, and they invest heavily in developing new measures that better illuminate key relationships. It is clear, however, that the future of HR will be characterized less by the lack of data than by questions about how to use data well and generate data judiciously.

Figure 1.1 shows, in three dimensions, how the HR consulting firm Towers Watson conveys the potential arenas of measurement. This figure illustrates the myriad ways in which HR can tackle its data. Being drowned in a sea of numbers is the problem; logic-driven analytics is the solution. The z-axis denotes the alternative business strategies an organization might pursue, whereas the x-axis captures the elements of the talent life cycle and the y-axis focuses on the four common categories of metrics. Each cell thus captures a unique set of metrics that are specific to the strategy, life cycle element, and type of

Figure 1.1 Data Measurement Framework

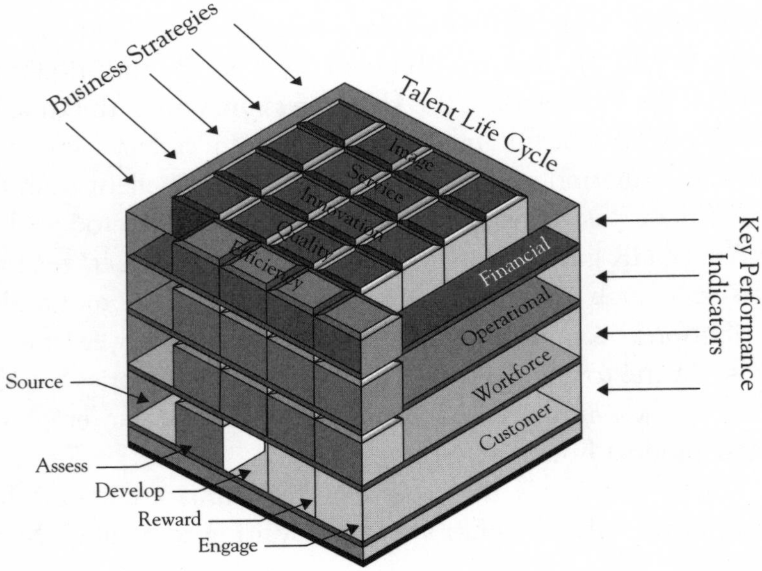

measurement focus for an organization. For example, a consumer goods company with an innovation-based strategy that is interested in employee metrics related to sourcing and selection might focus on the turnover of new hires in its product development group. A data cube like this helps organize data and metrics and identify the areas of focus.

Understanding Logic-Driven Analytics

The real crux of logic-driven analytics is that it is not enough to have numbers, and it is not enough to do an analysis of those numbers—there has to be an underlying logic guiding the analysis.

A typical HR metric is turnover. Turnover numbers are interesting. Add in an analysis of the cost of turnover, and the business begins to pay attention. Yet HR really begins to add value when it builds a logic around what is good turnover, what is bad turnover, and how the costs and benefits surrounding turnover can be optimized in light of business needs. This logic transforms the turnover metric from an interesting number into meaningful evidence that can guide the organization in making the right kinds of changes.

By *logic*, we are not implying the dry, formal methods taught in first-year philosophy. The term *logic* simply points to some context, some line of reasoning, that guides the analysis. In the example of the hospital (see the Introduction), the turnover numbers needed to be looked at in the context of what each department was delivering. There was a logic behind the relatively high turnover in the food service division. In light of that logic, it was possible to know whether the turnover was good or bad and whether any changes needed to be made. Without that logic, HR could not have seen what the numbers meant.

To help guide HR toward logic-driven analytics, Boudreau and Ramstad (2007) developed the *logic, analytics, measures, and process* (LAMP) mnemonic. The important point to remember is that *logic* comes first. Later in this book (see Chapter Nine), we will see how IBM captured numerous measures about the competencies of its consultants. This data capture was guided by the logic of viewing the talent pipeline as similar to a supply-chain pipeline, with the goal of having the right talent available to fill the business needs at the right time. Without the logical framework built on the supply-chain concept, IBM would have had a lot of metrics but no powerful metaphor to guide talent-management decisions on the basis of those data. High-quality measures and sophisticated analytics can reveal important insights, but evidence-based change often hinges on using the appropriate logic to target the analysis to the most promising and important questions.

In the Ameriprise case that also appears later in this book (see Chapter Ten), the issue was which HR services to continue to provide. One logical framework that was deployed was a marketing concept called *Kano analysis*; at its simplest, it involves distinguishing among the features that customers must have, the ones that they would like to have, and the ones that they do not expect but would be delighted to have. The logic used in this case guided thinking on what questions to ask and what data to collect about existing HR services. The company was able to collect all kinds of data about HR services—usage rates, user-satisfaction rates, figures for estimated impacts on sales, and so on—but in the absence of a logical framework such as Kano analysis, the company would have had just a collection of numbers, not a guide to decision making.

The *process* part of the LAMP framework is a critical but frequently overlooked aspect of logic-driven analytics. Good measures and analysis driven by a logical framework are not enough; there must be a process for communicating and framing the information in such a way that key constituents outside HR will act on it. Valid and insightful statistical analysis can add great value, but there is a danger that sophisticated statistical analysis by competent HR professionals can fall flat if it is seen as "HR speak." The same analysis can be a source of breakthrough change if carefully constructed to answer the right questions, and if presented in a way that makes it actionable by key decision makers. The latter outcome requires skills well beyond those of the typical data analyst or systems expert. IBM brought in a high-level supply-chain expert to help HR with the logic and assist with the process of communicating the implications to stakeholders.

Data and sophisticated analysis translate into true change leadership only when combined with the human touch. This calls for an individual or a group that brings an awareness of the audience, an ability to find the most significant relationships, an expert's eye for the organization's prominent mental models, and the insight of a good storyteller. Gebauer and Lowman (2008) share the compelling story of how McKesson combined data and analytics from multiple perspectives with leadership action to engage and involve employees in significantly enhancing the performance of the organization. It is this ability to use metrics thoughtfully in motivating and informing change that is at the heart of evidence-based change.

The "Analytics" in Logic-Driven Analytics

HR leaders are embracing the fact that skills in data collection and analysis are fundamental competencies for the HR profession. Analysis is sometimes the domain of a few specialists (note they are not necessarily in HR) with advanced degrees in such areas as psychology or economics. Nevertheless, the future of HR depends not only on such specialists but also on what is still the rare capacity for HR professionals to be at home with basic principles of data analysis, research design, and the statistical inferences that can and cannot be made from a set of data.

Here are a few principles of statistical and research design that are fundamental to a wide variety of human capital analyses but are often sources of error when they are ignored:

- *Sampling*, which makes it possible to generalize findings to the relevant situations
- *Correlation* (an instance of two phenomena tending to move in the same direction) as distinguished from *causality* (an instance of two phenomena moving together because one causes the other)
- Elimination of *alternative explanations* through careful design of experiments and quasi-experiments

None of these techniques requires an advanced degree in order to be used, and HR professionals need to take enough interest in these ideas to begin applying them to their work. Interested readers can learn more about these techniques by reading Cascio and Boudreau (2010) or by partnering with people who have experience in this area to grasp how these techniques are applied to HR analytics. However HR approaches learning these basic analytical tools, the takeaway is that they now belong in the toolkit of the typical HR professional; they are no longer just the purview of expert data analysts.

Another useful set of ideas about analytics is shown in Figure 1.2. In this figure, we see how Towers Watson thinks about the analytical domain in terms of the results of the analysis (the four rows) as they are applied to the main elements of the talent life cycle (the five columns). There are four sorts of analytical outcomes, represented by the rows labeled *Optimize*, *Predict*, *Correlate*, and *Describe and Benchmark*. With respect to the element labeled *Source and Select*, a starting point is simply to collect data, such as "cost per hire"—a *Describe and Benchmark* outcome. A more sophisticated approach is to undertake some analysis, such as correlating the quality of hires to business performance. As just noted, correlation should not be confused

Figure 1.2 Analytics at Each Phase of the Talent Life Cycle

	Source & Select	Assess	Develop & Deploy	Reward	Engage & Retain
	Measurement, Data Analytics, and Planning				
Optimize	• Model implementation of onboarding program and impact on sales per square foot	• Model implementation of performance management and impact on sales per square foot	• Model implementation of career development and impact on sales per square foot	• Model increased pay competitiveness and impact on sales per square foot	• Model impact of increased engagement through flexible scheduling on sales per square foot
Predict	• Predicted impact of reducing first-year turnover on percent change in sales per square foot	• Projected same-store revenue impact of greater percentage of high performers	• Projected impact on revenue/customer of increased managers per square foot	• Project impact of revenue/labor cost by a pay increase	• Projected sales per square foot by increasing engagement
Correlate	• Link new-hire engagement and customer satisfaction • Link first-year turnover—store manager and same-store revenue	• Link span of control—sales per square foot ratio to shrinkage	• Link percent of employees with a development plan to customer satisfaction and sales per square foot	• Link revenue/labor cost to percent change in same-store revenue • Link pay competitiveness to shrinkage	• Link engagement of store manager to sales per square foot
Describe & Benchmark	• New-hire engagement • First-year turnover—store manager • Cost per hire • Offer acceptance rate	• Performance distribution • Revenue per high-performing employee • Span of control—sales per square foot ratio	• Employee headcount • Sales per square foot/employee headcount • Percent of employees with a development plan • Sales per square foot/manager headcount	• Revenue/labor cost • Training cost per EE • Labor cost percentage of overall labor cost—store manager • Pay competitiveness	• Engagement • Store manager turnover • Absence rate—sales • Voluntary turnover by high performers • Internal staffing rate—first level managers

with causation, and a higher level of analysis seeks to predict causal outcomes on the basis of metrics (for example, one can predict the impact on productivity of a reduction in turnover among new hires). Finally, the most sophisticated outcome of analysis would be a model in which, for example, HR simulates the impact of investment in programs for new hires. The point is not that every analysis must strive for the upper part of the matrix, but rather that useful and change-inducing results can occur at every level of analysis. Where logic-driven analytics is concerned, HR needs to start applying frameworks like LAMP, learn the basics of data analysis, and be aware of the different levels of analysis, such as those shown in Figure 1.2, in order to act at the appropriate level.

HR analysts should also develop facility with a number of analytical concepts from economics and finance, including those listed here:

- The differences among fixed, variable, and operating costs
- The time value of money
- Present value and discounting
- The difference between cost-benefit analysis and cost-effectiveness analysis
- The notion of utility as the perceived value of something, where perceived value depends on the value of individual attributes, their probability, and their relationships
- The notion of break-even analysis and inflection points as opportunities for optimization and simplification

It is not our purpose to teach these concepts here but to draw attention to the idea that logic-driven analytics rests, in part, on the strength and validity of the analysis itself. These concepts are not overly difficult, and the easiest way to learn how to apply them to HR issues is to partner with people in the business to whom these concepts are second nature.

That said, as we noted earlier, even the most rigorous analysis that uses the most valid measures can fail to induce change if it is not carefully crafted with the use of logical frameworks that engage the target audiences.

Using Logic to Find the Right "Story"

Organizations have the potential to generate thousands of reports on such issues as turnover, employee attitudes, and skill levels, and to parse the data so as to give personal reports to leaders in every unit, reports that can be further analyzed for all sorts of associations. It might be discovered, for instance, that turnover in one unit is higher among females early in their careers, or that employee attitudes are below national benchmark levels in units that fail to meet their financial goals. Again, however, the goal is not simply to generate interesting HR metrics and analysis but to use analytics to make good decisions and drive change. That distinction bears repeating when the HR function in so many organizations makes the mistake of simply throwing data out to its constituents, in the hope that they will make the necessary connections to important outcomes, root causes, and actions that will produce results.

Thus one important use of logic is to discern which data and which analytics are likely to be most pivotal to the vital issues facing the organization. That's why HR analysts have to be good at analyzing strategy and business issues and understanding how human capital connects to those issues. Although these skills are similar to what is typically described as business acumen in today's competency models, they go well beyond business acumen. Here, we are talking about the ability to understand the logic of the business well enough to see where data about human capital can most improve decisions that will have a pivotal impact on important business results.

For example, if the logic of the business says that selling more to existing customers is more profitable than acquiring new customers, then HR data reflecting the first goal should be the focus of the business decision makers. It is not enough simply to show that more employee engagement is associated with higher sales; it is also necessary to show how engagement relates to *existing-customer* sales. Thus the logic of the business drives HR to ask, "What kinds of employee attitudes drive improved sales to existing customers? What HR programs improve those attitudes?" Data and analysis that provide answers to those questions will create a very compelling story, which is also vital to key decisions, whereas more generic data about employee attitudes and HR programs can fail to direct attention to the pivot points. This is where data cubes like the one shown in Figure 1.1 can be useful. They help create the connective tissue between the strategic and operational aspects of the business and the requirements for the various aspects of the talent life cycle.

In the future, however, the value of understanding logic will go beyond making HR leaders savvier about understanding and communicating connections between their analyses and the business. In next-generation HR, logic will actually be able to enhance the credibility of results because it will be connected with frameworks that leaders already use.

Using Logic to Create an Emotional Connection

Mr. Spock, the *Star Trek* character, is known for his dispassionate application of logic, to the exclusion of all emotion, and yet episode after episode of this TV series shows that it is often an emotional connection to his logical arguments that creates the catalyst for great achievements. In the real world as well, this lesson is profound and is often the source of the most perplexing aspects of HR analysis and data.

Many HR units and HR data analysts are frustrated because they know that their analytical work is first-rate, and they even see it published in prestigious scientific journals. But decades of evidence suggest that managers seldom read such journals, know very little about this kind of scientific evidence, and routinely ignore findings that most human behavior scientists would regard as well documented. One reason for this paradox is that HR analysis aimed exclusively at scientific rigor often fails to connect with the context and reality of the problems the analysis is designed to address. In organizations, this failure displays itself as a tendency for leaders to listen politely to and even applaud HR analysis but then place the findings on a shelf, never to consult them again.

The cases you will read about in this book show how a number of HR leaders overcame this tendency. The cases also show how leading organizations have deftly embedded rigorous analysis within logic models and frameworks that are familiar to key constituents. We have already mentioned that IBM drew on a supply-chain metaphor; later in this chapter, you will see how Deutsche Telekom used the same metaphor to reframe the logic of succession and leadership development. These frameworks are effective because stakeholders understand them and trust them. When analysis is framed in a comfortable way, stakeholders do not just listen; they take action, and they embed the logic of the analysis in their decisions. Boudreau (2010) coined the term *retooling HR* to describe this kind of framing, offering examples that involve retooling turnover data within a framework of inventory

Assessing Your Level of Analytical Sophistication

Cascio and Boudreau (2010) have suggested a continuum of analytical sophistication that can be used to get a sense of how far along you are in the world of logic-driven analytics:

1. *Counting: making sure all the relevant data about the workforce are tracked, organized, and accessible.* For example, HR will

(Continued)

have ready access to facts like the number of senior jobs filled internally. This sounds straightforward, but a lot of work is involved in getting to this first stage.

2. *Clever counting: extrapolating from descriptive data to yield insights through trend projections or cross-group comparisons.* For example, analysis may show that Asian leaders are more likely to be promoted into senior jobs than are European leaders, a practice that is likely to result in a narrow range of perspectives at the top of the organization.

3. *Insight: understanding the drivers behind the trends and cross-group differences discovered through clever counting.* For example, HR will recognize that the way Asian leaders are developed through cross-unit assignments better prepares them for senior jobs, thus clarifying the root cause of their disproportionate promotion numbers and suggesting possible solutions.

4. *Influence: using analytical results to create valuable and tangible change.* For example, HR will personalize the overall data in a way that grabs the CEO's attention by showing individual cases of good European leaders who left because they correctly perceived that there was little room for their advancement. It is the evolution toward *influence* that is the hallmark of well-integrated logic and analysis, the heart of logic-driven analytics.

Sometimes organizations invest inordinate effort in mastering the *clever counting* stage and fall short on *insight* and *influence*. (But see Chapter Eleven for a description of how the Royal Bank of Scotland [RBS] Group quite consciously aimed for *insight* and *influence* rather than building the world's best HR data warehouse.) This simple continuum should help you assess the sophistication of logic-driven analytics in your organization.

turnover, reframing talent sourcing and assessment validity within the frameworks of supply chains and quality control, and reframing leadership readiness for an uncertain future within the framework of financial portfolio theory and risk hedging.

"Back of the Envelope" Versus Pushing the Envelope

In an age when it will be ever easier to generate numbers and statistical analysis about your workforce, perhaps the most important principle to keep in mind is that less is often more. The cases in this book certainly offer insights into advanced and forward-thinking data and analysis systems, and it is easy to become frustrated if your organization isn't blessed with such an advanced infrastructure or with a cadre of advanced technical analysts. Nevertheless, to fixate on these things is to miss a fundamental point: namely, logic-driven analytics is about creating *evidence-based change*, not necessarily about creating the most impressive data system or analysis.

The sophistication of the analysis should be consistent with the best way to create the needed change. If you read carefully, you will find that in many of the cases featured in this book, the most important "data" were not numerical at all but instead statistics personalized by using a real example or statistics translated into a logical story. By scientific standards, the actual calculations were often imprecise, but they were compelling enough to get attention and generate action. Logic-driven analytics requires enough precision to avoid mistakes, but that does not usually mean pushing the envelope to the limits of the technology. "Back of the envelope" is often enough—and can be even more effective.

Deutsche Telekom: Bringing the Logic of the Supply Chain to the Analytics of Leadership

How do most organizations make decisions on succession? Is it a smooth process, or is HR scrambling at the last minute to source an external candidate or promote someone not quite ready for the job? Leaders often feel certain that *somewhere* in the company, there must be someone able to do the job—or at least someone who could have been ready with better planning. Then they reluctantly search outside.

Recognition that we need to plan for succession leads to the appropriately named *succession planning process*, which typically requires identifying a successor for each key position. Unfortunately, this often becomes an administrative "name-to-box" exercise. Yes, this way a possible successor is named. But it involves one name only, without strong evidence this person is the best choice, nor is there good data about the candidate's readiness to move up, let alone about what has been done to prepare him or her. In many organizations, fewer than 50 percent of those promoted were actually listed on the succession plan for the position. Furthermore, name-to-box succession plans do not address the broader issue of developing deep talent pipelines enterprisewide.

Deutsche Telekom (DT) "retooled" the challenges of succession planning to those of building talent pipelines. They realized that essentially the problem was one of logic-driven analytics. They needed good-quality data about their talent across the enterprise, and they needed to analyze it based on a legitimate logical framework of pipelines. Additionally, they had to present it with a logic framework that would engage leaders outside HR to make good decisions about promotions, deployment, and development. This case shows how DT solved the problem of generating the right data and making it useful, all the while generating buy-in from all key stakeholders. It reveals how systematic attention to creating common logic frameworks, then using them to direct data analysis and presentation, leads naturally to more positive outcomes for HR systems.

Understanding Deutsche Telekom's Situation

DT is a global telecommunications and information technology company with operations in 50 countries. A big organization with

260,000 employees, it has many lines of business—broadband, fixed-network services, mobile communications, and Internet TV. The business units are extremely strong, and most are very profitable, so enterprisewide initiatives must be acceptable to these powerful stakeholders.

The telecommunications industry is fast-moving and talent-driven. Therefore, it is no surprise DT felt it needed a steering tool to allow leadership to assess the balance between demand for and supply of talent in pivotal areas. In the past, DT had faced situations where it was simultaneously laying off large numbers of people in one division while hiring large numbers in another. This raised the question of whether it would have been possible to redeploy people instead. But that sort of redeployment is not possible without a good enterprisewide talent-management system.

While there may have been a fair bit of talent management going on at DT, every business unit did things differently. Each unit had its own database for talent, with its own structure, definitions, tracking systems, and protocols. Even if one unit tried looking across to other units for openings for its surplus people, or to find available talent to fill a vacancy, the need to reconcile different systems would stymie the search. Not only that, but in many cases the same role had different titles or definitions in different units. Naturally, leaders tended to stick to the data and analysis systems they knew, which often meant considering talent only in their units. Like an inventory system trying to reconcile the pipeline of materials, unfinished goods, and production without a common logical framework, data, and analysis, it is not possible to achieve the synergies that cross-unit integration can bring. Until they tackled the problem at an enterprise level, it was impossible to have any kind of overall picture of talent pipelines at DT.

Creating Buy-In and Developing a Logical Framework

Why would there be resistance to a new system for developing talent pipelines? Ironically, one issue was that the business units really cared about talent. They tended to see talent as their own property, not an enterprisewide resource. They were concerned that any enterprisewide system would mean they could lose their best talent to other units. Furthermore, because they cared about talent, they had their own ways of assessing competencies and determining readiness. The business units thought any new system would not be as effective in meeting their needs as their homegrown systems. To get the business units onside, HR needed to show that any new system served all stakeholders well, and that the benefits of cross-unit cooperation outweighed the costs.

The most important first step is what HR did *not* do—they did not go off and design a state-of-the-art talent-management system and *then* try to get buy-in. Instead they held a monthly stakeholder meeting where stakeholders were part of the development process.

Since the new system would need to be as good for the business units as what they had in place, the starting point was to research all the existing databases and frameworks to assess talent (for example, methods for assessing performance, competencies, and potential) and how those systems addressed talent requirements of each specific business need. As the stakeholders looked at the different systems, they could see unique advantages of each and then consider how those systems might contribute to the common goal of excellent talent. This perspective allowed them to imagine what the right practice for the enterprise would be.

Most important, their research extended beyond HR professionals in the business units to interviews with line managers and the board about needed outputs from the talent-management system. This meant that in stakeholder meetings, HR could lead good evidence-based discussions on what managers and the board wanted; it avoided a descent into a "we like this" versus "you like that" argument. Knowing what the board wants is a powerful means for forging agreement across units because it can focus attention on the organization-wide outcomes as well as best outcomes for individual units. The board's involvement helped emphasize that competent talent was a critical corporate asset, not just a means for business unit heads to achieve their own goals.

The final step was to build the new approach to talent in a way that integrated with what was currently in place so it was easy for business units to migrate to a common system that would provide them an organization-wide perspective.

Sometimes getting buy-in is seen as selling an idea to someone. But as DT demonstrates, with an evidence-based approach, getting buy-in can be about getting stakeholders to engage in a process of learning about different approaches and reaching a conclusion together. DT used evidence to inform a logical premise—that the objective was achieving optimal balance between common and standardized systems that allow cross-unit talent movement with systems individualized and customized enough to meet particular unit needs.

Thinking About Talent Analytics

For effective talent management, DT needed information about the current quality and quantity of talent—what would be in the new talent management system; future supply—what it could project based on reasonable assumptions about attrition and development; and future demand for talent—which would be an output of the company's business planning processes.

To populate a system with data about the quantity and quality of talent, there needs to be a common language about the levels, job families, and competencies across the enterprise. The most important tool was a common taxonomy of about 60 job families, each of which comprised a number of subfamilies. For example, HR was a job family with subfamilies such as HR Development and HR Business Partner. This taxonomy provided enough detail that any unit could look across the enterprise to find potential candidates, but not so much detail that the system became unwieldy. Now if a leader in the Chinese operations needed to fill a position in a certain subfamily of finance, he or she could easily search across the whole organization to see what talent was available.

This setup offered room for business units to customize aspects of the system to their own needs—for example, using some of their own competencies. However, wherever it made sense, there was enterprisewide consistency. For instance, at the top three levels of management there is a single competency model for all of DT, because once leaders reached the top three management levels, the highest priority for the system was ability to develop and deploy those leaders across the enterprise. The top three management levels are clearly seen as a "corporate asset." Similarly, all units use the same method for describing the quality of talent, using the familiar dimensions of performance and potential, where potential is based on a competency analysis (Figure 1.3). The common framework makes it possible to talk about talent in the same language across different business units, and if a unit has many high potentials/high performers, then it would be natural to export some to other units.

An important additional assessment for each employee is shown in Figure 1.4. It is common for a measure of potential to

Figure 1.3 Performance Versus Potential: Matrix for an Individual

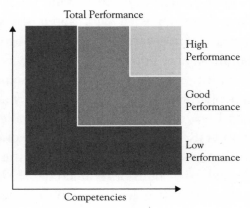

Figure 1.4 Readiness for Vertical or Horizontal Movement

Job Families		
Horizontal	Vertical	Job Families
☐	✓	Management
☐	☐	Corporate
✓	☐	Technology
☐	☐	Finance
☐	☐	IT
☐	☐	HR
☐	☐	Marketing/Product Management
☐	☐	Sales

show whether individuals are ready to move up vertically in their job family, but DT added assessing which other job families they might be able to move to horizontally. For example, the figure shows an individual with tick marks showing that not only can that person move up vertically in the Management job family but that he or she has also the ability to move horizontally into Technology.

The addition of this horizontal perspective opened up the potential for the organization to move talent around in a way that fills gaps and deflates surpluses. This was a new way of thinking for managers accustomed to thinking of talent deployment and development only within their unit and in an upward direction. It was difficult at first, but has now become an essential piece of data for making good decisions about deployment and identifying when talent gaps can be filled by a combination of vertical and horizontal moves instead of going outside to hire. A subtle change in the logical model of talent movement (adding consideration of horizontal moves), combined with additional data showing where individuals might be ready for a horizontal move, revealed talent management options that had been hidden. Whether the issue is staffing, reorganization, or downsizing common job families, the data on horizontal mobility make it easy to see options available to the organization. All this is mediated by a common technology infrastructure that ensures a search for talent automatically brings up people from other units who could potentially fill an opening.

"Lately, we moved one of our HR talents from HR to the internal auditing department; this would not have been possible without transparency regarding her personal career plans. The tool simply helps us to create more opportunities," said Torsten Bittlingmaier, Head of Corporate Talent Management.

From Data to Decisions

An essential step in any analytics approach is to ensure that the data can be presented to leaders in a way that will help them make decisions. In the case of DT, the main tool was a traffic light graphic (see Figure 1.5), which showed whether a talent pipeline was strong (green light), acceptable (yellow light), or weak (red light). The information could be shown by management level and job function. This graphic was quite easy for the managing board to read and nicely drew the board's attention to any foreseen talent deficits in critical areas. A "more info" button would drill down to provide detail in any segment, such as how many high potentials there were, how many high performers, how many solid performers, the gender distribution, the age distribution, and other key performance indicators for the pool. It was really easy to see the talent landscape, and the system itself is simple to use. The ease of analysis leads to well-informed decisions on whether to hire, redeploy, or retrain. For example, if there were a yellow light in Finance at the Group 1 level, HR could look more closely at the supply options of moving people up more quickly or moving people laterally into the function (with appropriate training). If the gap still could not be adequately addressed, then they would know it was time to start looking to external hires. This

Figure 1.5 Traffic Light to Highlight Talent Shortfalls

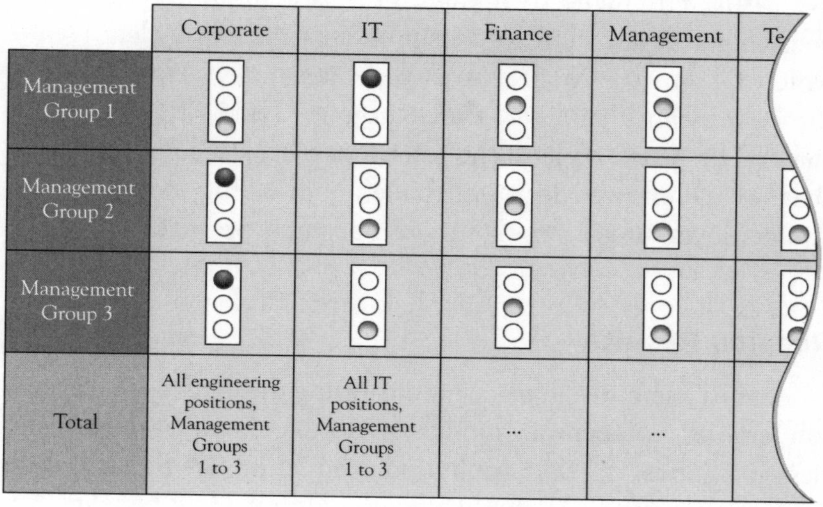

	Corporate	IT	Finance	Management	Te
Management Group 1	○○●	●○○	○○○	○○○	
Management Group 2	●○○	○○○	○○○	○○○	○○
Management Group 3	●○○	○○○	○○○	○○○	○○
Total	All engineering positions, Management Groups 1 to 3	All IT positions, Management Groups 1 to 3	...	...	

is a much broader and longer-term view of talent than is often the case in other firms, where only when a vacancy has already occurred, the shallowness of the talent pool is revealed. "We expect the traffic lights to alert us proactively and give us the opportunity to take necessary actions before issues become crises," said Bittlingmaier.

To review the talent pool data and to derive actions accordingly, two process steps were introduced—the succession meeting and the talent review. Each business unit conducts a succession meeting that focuses on reviewing the data as well as conducting an additional name-to-box succession planning for critical roles. Naturally, this meeting is more oriented toward risk management. The talent review is conducted by job family and aimed at increasing transparency across business units. In this meeting the pipeline is reviewed, and bench strength is discussed for the job family. These meetings allowed DT to actively manage its talent pipeline and react to upcoming talent shortages.

The board really likes the system, in no small part because it means that HR is well connected to the business strategy. If the business will need certain kinds of talent in the next three to five years, HR focuses on that. This is a natural goal, but in many organizations HR runs its programs without a clear idea of which talent issues matter most to leadership. Getting HR data the board wants, in a way they can make sense of, changes the game. The board reviews the talent map on a regular basis, and that review ensures decisions made about hiring, development, and deployment are consistent with business priorities.

Reaping Results

Once the system was in place for organizing the data—standardized job families, competency models, performance ratings and readiness categories, the data itself, and the technology to gather and present the data—DT could reap a wide range of benefits. For example, the company could:

- Start with the business plan to determine the quantity and quality of talent (using the job family taxonomy) required to execute that plan over a multiyear period, and then compare that to the supply of talent and plan accordingly
- Initiate job rotations within or across business units
- Deploy "excess" talent where it was most needed
- Ensure there was a robust pipeline of talent for critical positions

A more straightforward benefit is that, because the organization now has a good handle on where talent shortages and surpluses will be, HR can equip managers to give much better advice on where career opportunities will be. Historically, managers might have a nice discussion with an employee about what he or she would like to do, but then nothing would come of it because no vacancies existed in that area. Now such discussions can be based on facts, not wishful thinking. If someone in IT is interested in an HR career, now it is possible to give that person a realistic assessment of the openings expected in the HR job family, enterprisewide, in the next few years.

Similarly, a problem with high-potential employees is that they always have an expectation that a promotion is right around the corner. With the talent-management system in place, HR and managers had the data they needed to manage expectations much more realistically. For example, if their forecasts showed there would be vacancies in the individual's job family, then HR could accurately inform a high potential that rapid movement was likely. If the job family was already well staffed or demand would be shrinking due to changes in the business strategy, then the individual could be given the realistic view that there were unlikely to be openings soon. And, of course, that could naturally lead to looking more seriously at possible lateral moves into job families where demand would be higher. These improvements in career planning, as well as the enhanced opportunity for cross-unit moves, supported DT's efforts to continue to build its brand as a great place to have a productive career.

DT has shown that talent management is not an imprecise art form. Rather, it is a rigorous science based on solid numbers that tie to strategy. This enterprisewide view helped dissolve the parochialism of the business units and demonstrate the value of managing talent as a corporate resource. This case is an excellent example of how an analytic mind-set approaches a complex problem and not only builds an effective system but gets buy-in as the system develops.

The One Thing You Should Take Away

Although good measures and the right analysis are important, getting the numbers right is just the beginning. The magic happens when the measures and analysis are combined with the logic to know where to look for the important connections and the savvy to know when a story is better than a number and a good metaphor is better than yet another spreadsheet.

2

WHERE ARE YOUR PIVOTAL TALENT SEGMENTS?

Segmentation is about discovering the strategic categories of employees and potential employees by understanding the most vital differences between them. These strategic categories are based on what the organization needs from employees and potential employees (demand side) or on what the organization can offer to attract or motivate them (supply side). Identifying these differences allows an organization to craft unique deals that meet the needs of particular segments and to target those deals to the segments where they will have the biggest impact.

Segmentation, a central framework of marketing, ought to be a central framework for HR as well. In marketing, segmentation means dividing the population of customers and potential customers into groups, deciding which ones to target, and then customizing the product, its pricing, and its positioning to best serve those target groups. Segmentation strikes an optimal balance between the efficiency of standardization and the responsiveness of customization. In a resource-constrained world, the same principle of understanding and optimizing the value exchange between the organization and different groups is also essential to business performance with respect to employees or potential employees.

How do we bring that kind of thinking to HR?

HR has long supported and enabled individual differentiation on the basis of performance and/or potential. But the principle of segmenting groups of employees is a newer concept. From an HR perspective, there are two different types of segmentation:

- *Segmentation of the workforce according to the employment features that attract or motivate a certain group.* We call this *supply-side segmentation* because it defines the "deal" that will cause employees and potential employees to "supply" such things as joining, performing for, and staying with the organization. A great example of supply-side segmentation is illustrated in the case of Shanda Interactive Entertainment, Limited (see Chapter Four). Shanda focused on a segment of employees and potential employees defined within a certain age group—twenty-somethings in China—and, after analyzing their wants and needs, created a specific, customized deal to attract and retain talent from this particular demographic group.

- *Segmentation of the workforce and of work according to what the organization needs from employees.* We call this *demand-side segmentation* because it defines actions and behaviors that the organization "demands" from employees—joining, performing, and staying. These are the actions that will contribute most to the organization's success. This kind of segmentation is described in the case of CME Group, presented at the end of this chapter. CME Group developed an understanding of the specific job "segments" in which improvements in performance were pivotal to executing its new strategy and to driving growth. The essence of demand-side segmentation for CME Group was defining performance elements that were pivotal.

Shanda and CME Group combined supply-side and demand-side segmentation to craft nuanced talent strategies designed to attract and motivate specific talent segments. In this way, each of them optimized the value exchange between talent and the organization—both sides got what they wanted. The same segmentation principles were applied in both cases, but the specific outcomes in each organization were quite different.

Thinking about segmentation takes HR down a logic path that can affect virtually every aspect of the employee value proposition and the talent life cycle—for instance, how talent is selected for various jobs, how high-potential talent is deployed, and how employees in different roles are rewarded. Although the idea of segmentation sounds obvious, HR traditionally has taken a "peanut butter" approach to talent, by which HR investments are similar—spread like peanut butter—across different roles and employee groups. That is, if innovation is an issue, then everyone gets training in being innovative, and if diversity is an issue, then every leader has to find a way to increase diversity scores, and if machinists get flextime, then that benefit goes to all hourly employees throughout the organization. Segmentation, however, invites a different way of thinking by focusing on how employees with certain attributes or behaviors (such as diversity or innovation) might, in different roles, affect strategic success differently, and on how employment features (such as hours, pay, or development) might affect individual behaviors differently across different groups. As in marketing, once these distinctions are understood, they can reveal ways to invest differently across employee segments to achieve more optimal results. Segmentation is about understanding the differences between groups, whereas optimization is about using that information to make investment decisions.

HR leaders can use the following three fundamental questions from marketing and consumer research to analyze, evaluate, and communicate strategic talent-supply decisions:

1. What are our vital talent segments?
2. Which employment elements induce the desired responses at optimum cost (supply-side talent segmentation)?
3. What do we need employees to do (demand-side talent segmentation)?

Supply-Side Segmentation

Supply-side talent segmentation focuses on differences in what motivates vital behaviors—joining, performing, staying, and so on—among applicants or employees. Supply-side segmentation requires, first, identification of strategically relevant talent segments. Second, it requires an understanding of which features of the employment relationship motivate behaviors. For example, an organization might identify "people willing to travel frequently" as an important talent segment for certain jobs. It could then craft an attractive employment deal for this talent segment— perhaps longer vacation time. This employment deal need not apply to everyone, just to the segment where it is needed to attract the right talent. The traditional approach is to consider changing employees' vacation time across the board because doing so may make the organization more attractive in a general way, but the segmentation approach changes the deal in a specific way for a specific segment for a specific reason.

As Boudreau (2010) has noted, marketing principles suggest that talent-supply segments can be identified if the following six factors are considered:

1. *Identifiability*, the degree of ease in using vital attributes to describe the segment as a distinct group

2. *Substantiality*, the size of the segment and its potential impact on profitability

3. *Accessibility*, the degree to which an organization can reach the segment through communication, promotion, and distribution

4. *Responsiveness*, the predictability, uniqueness, and strength of the response to a strategy on the part of individuals in the segment

5. *Stability*, the length of time that members of the segment will keep responding, and determination of whether that is long enough to justify implementation of the strategy

6. *Actionability*, the degree to which actions taken to satisfy those in the segment are feasible and consistent with the organization's goals, values, and competencies

As in marketing, where companies decide which consumer segments to pursue, organizations making decisions about talent have choices about how many talent segments they will pursue and how aggressively they will pursue them. A company may choose to craft a product-value proposition that generically appeals to almost everyone, and in the talent domain such a proposition would include such attributes as fairness, competitive rewards, career opportunities, and so on. Some companies—for instance, those producing luxury-brand products, such as Louis Vuitton or Prada—craft highly specific and exclusive value propositions, and they focus their product, marketing, and branding efforts uniquely on a specific consumer segment, taking the calculated risk that many other consumers may find their messages less appealing. This approach also applies to the talent world, particularly in small organizations that clearly stand or fall on the quality of one talent segment, such as biotechnology scientists or software engineers. An employee value proposition aimed at scientists might not be optimal at attracting employees for the other jobs in the organization, but that drawback is more than compensated for by the ability to fill the pivotal roles.

A variation on crafting an exclusive single-value proposition is crafting a value proposition that is specific but relevant to almost all roles. For example, Boudreau and Ramstad (2007) have described how Williams-Sonoma created a value proposition built on working to create fashion-forward household products. This approach meant that the organization was an employer of choice for jobs involving product design, merchandising, and customer relations. Supply-side attractiveness to people working in these job segments was a natural by-product of this approach. Yet, on the face of it, such an approach was less likely to attract the Web designers and engineers that the company needed as it embarked on an Internet-channel strategy in the late 1990s; Williams-Sonoma found that most technical professionals were more drawn to organizations like Microsoft, Yahoo! and Apple, which promised the latest technology and an engineering-driven culture. Surprisingly, however, Williams-Sonoma did turn out to be attractive to a particular subsegment of technical professionals—Web designers and engineers with a particular interest in brands, fashion, and product design. Indeed, such technical professionals were a better fit for the demand-side needs of Williams-Sonoma because they were more likely to be motivated to apply their technical capabilities to the arenas of fashion and brands. When we apply the six marketing principles listed earlier to Williams-Sonoma's talent segment of technical professionals in Web design and engineering who were also interested in fashion and brands, we see that their characteristics were as follows:

1. *Identifiable:* The company was able to identify this distinct group, even though at first this segment was obscured by the company's temptation to look only at technical skills.

2. *Substantial:* The organization realized that it needed only a small number of such professionals, and that focusing its segmentation on those most compatible with the company could actually yield high quality and sufficient quantity.

3. *Accessible:* The company realized that many of these professionals were quite aware of the company; no great effort to attract them was required, once it was known that the company had a need for them.

4. *Responsive:* These types of technical professionals were much more likely to apply, join, stay, and work effectively than were technical professionals with less interest in fashion and brands.

5. *Stable:* This segment was likely to remain interested in fashion and brands over time.

6. *Actionable:* It took far less to attract, retain, and reward this subset than it would have taken to attract technical professionals without an interest in fashion and brands, and so the company's efforts to target this segment were very efficient.

For HR and organizational leaders, the emerging requirement will be to strike the right balance in establishing multiple value propositions while avoiding the inefficiency and chaos of customizing the deal for every individual or particular talent segment. Thus the emerging requirement will probably be quite similar to the marketing challenge faced by companies in pursuit of consumers. The six principles noted earlier can help an organization approach supply-side segmentation more rationally.

Demand-Side Segmentation

It would not seem odd to hear a leader say, "We need to get the best from all our people and help them improve all their competencies." Yet that same leader would never make a similar comment about customers: "We must provide the best possible service on all service dimensions for every customer."

It is impossible to fully serve the needs of every customer. Choices must be made. Consider the world of a global hospitality chain. Although it serves the needs of all patrons, the chain is acutely aware of the unique needs of those customers—its premium guests—who are most critical to driving its revenues. Someone who stays fifty times a year experiences a different level of service from that extended to a guest who stays only once a year.

The economics justify offering these differentiated service levels. The payoff for getting frequent-stayers to shift 10 percent of their lodging choices to one particular hotel can translate into many thousands of dollars per year; likewise, the cost of losing 10 percent of their total lodging business can cost many thousands of dollars per year. There is value in attracting less-frequent-stayers, and it is regrettable if their business is lost to a competitor, but the economic consequences are far less serious.

The principle of demand-side segmentation for talent rests on similar logic. Just as it is not economically logical for a hospitality chain to try to provide the highest level of service to frequent- and occasional-stayers alike, it is often not economically optimal for progressive HR functions to achieve "top performance" or acquire "the very best talent" in every role. A more optimal approach is to understand how various talent roles contribute to strategic success. This kind of demand-side segmentation can then be combined with supply-side segmentation to create employment deals with an optimal value exchange.

Return on Improved Performance

A powerful tool for demand-side segmentation is the performance-yield curve. This kind of graph clearly articulates the return on improved performance (ROIP) of a particular role or job—that is, the degree to which performance improvement in that role or job creates higher value for the organization.

There is a difference between saying that a role is important and saying that a role is pivotal, and that difference is what lies at the heart of the ROIP concept. A role's importance has to do with the average value created by that role; thus the role of corporate controller may add more value, and hence be more *important*, than the role of R&D scientist. At the same time, the role of controller may be less *pivotal* than the role of R&D scientist, which is to say that improvement in the controller's performance may not add much value to the organization, whereas improvement in the R&D scientist's performance may have a big impact. Therefore, an organization might do well to acquire a 90th-percentile performer in the R&D scientist role and be satisfied with a 50th-percentile performer in the controller role. When we talk about pivotal jobs, then, we mean jobs whose ROIP is very high. Most HR structures today are extremely good at segmenting an organization hierarchically (that is, on the basis of the importance or average value of roles), but few are good at segmenting on the basis of how pivotal roles are.

As we have just seen, differences in ROIP may appear when existing roles are compared. Differences may also appear when the subelements of a job are examined, as when one element of performance has to meet a particular standard (but need not be higher), whereas other performance elements add more value the more they improve. Using ROIP to identify demand-side segments can also reveal pivotal job elements or roles that don't yet exist in the organization's job or performance system. For example, Boudreau (2010) discusses Boeing's commercial aircraft engineers, whose enhanced skills in aluminum-based technologies had historically increased the organization's value. With Boeing's decision to pursue production of the 787 aircraft, built of composite materials, and to rely much more on suppliers for key technical knowledge, the pivotal job element for the company's commercial aircraft engineers shifted from skills in aluminum-based technologies to the ability to work effectively with suppliers of composite materials. That particular job element probably had not been emphasized in these engineers' traditional job description, and so their experience highlights the difference between the pivotal performance elements in a current role and those performance elements that will become pivotal in the future.

Figures 2.1 and 2.2 illustrate how the concept of ROIP can be used to identify demand-side talent segments. The figures represent two key roles at a commercial airline—pilot and flight attendant—with value to the organization defined in terms of the customer experience. (The analysis that follows is based on Towers Watson's adaptation of Boudreau's work as applied to a number of major airlines.)

Figure 2.1 ROIP Curve for a Flight Attendant

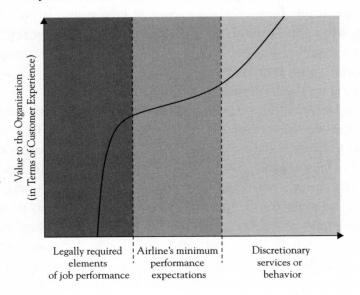

In Figure 2.1, the ROIP curve for the regulated position of flight attendant reflects three key aspects of that role:

1. An aspect that addresses the services legally required by regulators (think of the various safety procedures)
2. An aspect that captures the basic job expectations of the particular airline (for example, providing in-flight beverage service)
3. An aspect that is discretionary (for example, problem solving)

Although each of these three aspects of the role can be plotted as a unique curve, they actually build on each other when viewed through the lens of value to the customer (note, for example, that the value to the customer of the legally required aspects of the job is lower than the value of the airline's basic expectations for a flight attendant).

In the left-hand portion of this figure, the curve rises quickly because any failure to carry out legally required procedures may cause accidents or result in fines, but once the flight attendant's performance has met the legal standard, there is little value in exceeding that standard.

In the middle portion of the figure, the curve rises because the expected services do contribute to passengers' comfort and satisfaction. Nevertheless, they are expected, and if they are delivered within the expected range, they largely go unnoticed.

In the right-hand portion of the figure, the curve slopes sharply upward. Consider that the flight attendant is the face of the company for 60 to 90 percent of the average premium passenger's total flying experience, from the time the passenger arrives at the airport to the time he deplanes at his destination and picks up his baggage. Clearly, the flight attendant's role is pivotal in helping the airline deliver on the unique promise of its brand and in ensuring the retention of the passenger, who in turn is essential to the organization's economic well-being. Given all this "face time" with passengers, many airlines look to the flight attendant role to drive additional revenue opportunities (sales of onboard meals and amenities, duty-free goods, and so on). Thus the organization stands to reap big payoffs from investing in flight attendants and getting them as far as possible into the performance dimension represented by the top right portion of Figure 2.1.

Figure 2.2 compares the ROIP curves for a flight attendant and a pilot. Not surprisingly, the legally required elements of a pilot's performance, represented by the curve in the left-hand portion of the figure, rise to a much higher level than do those for a flight attendant. In the middle portion of the figure, however, the pilot's ROIP curve quickly flattens out because there is minimal incremental value, either to the organization or to the customer, associated with having pilots exceed the basic requirements of the job (taking off on time, flying safely, and minimizing in-flight incidents). Consider that the pilot is the face of the company for

Figure 2.2 Comparison of ROIP Curves for a Flight Attendant and a Pilot

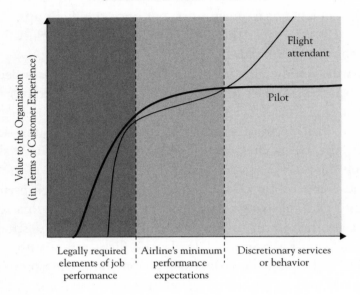

less than 1 percent of the passenger's total flying experience. If the pilot comes out of the cockpit and personally greets the first-class passengers, that may be a memorable occasion, but it does nothing that specifically shapes the premium flyer's experience (and it could even be an irritant for a passenger trying to get some work completed during those precious quiet moments on board the plane). Thus it is also not surprising that in the right-hand portion of the figure, the ROIP curve for the flight attendant quickly rises above that of the pilot.

Table 2.1 presents the implications for HR investments in these two job families—flight attendant and pilot—that have different ROIP patterns with respect to the customer experience. The logic of differentiating these investments is self-evident when it is viewed through the lens of the ROIP curve. Clearly, HR investments should be differentiated on the basis of how pivotal the talent is in each job family. Nevertheless, organizations routinely develop one-size-fits-all solutions for the entire

Table 2.1 Flight Attendant and Pilot: Implications for HR Investments

Flight Attendant	Pilot
Sourcing and development: Significant premium placed on talent with critical competencies in customer service, including talent from other industries, such as retail	*Sourcing and development:* Emphasis on recruiting talent early in career, with an emphasis on apprenticeship and a long development cycle to encourage the acquisition of experience and skills (as often happens in military service before talent joins a commercial airline)
Performance management and rewards: Aggressive differentiation of individual performance on the basis of service provided (performance-based incentives would encourage individuals to move farther along the performance curve)	*Performance management and rewards:* Minimal differentiation of individual performance (which might encourage risk taking) or use of performance-based incentives; emphasis on steadily increasing rewards as skills are acquired and as talent progresses through the organization

workforce. Such solutions not only risk the waste of resources but also encourage counterproductive behavior (for example, offering incentives that encourage pilots to take risks when in fact pilots should be encouraged to operate within the flat portions of the curve).

Making Segmentation Happen

The logic of segmentation is self-evident, but that does not mean it is without its challenges. Does providing customer service–related performance incentives more aggressively to flight attendants than to pilots mean that pilots are somehow less important or respected than flight attendants? No. It is a signal that the best thing for everyone's collective success and employment is to have flight attendants emphasize customer service more heavily and have pilots concentrate on adhering to strict performance standards in the vital arena of flight safety. As in anything else related to people, HR needs to strike the right balance. Few organizations will create large numbers of different deals for the workforce on the basis of talent segmentation. The costs and implementation challenges would be too great. Nevertheless, to err on the side of too much standardization will also cause a company to miss valuable opportunities.

We may worry that segmentation might upset employees because HR would seem to be saying that one group is more pivotal than another, or that one skill now matters more than another. But it is worth remembering that we have fought this battle before. As noted by Boudreau and Ramstad (2007), organizations now routinely treat high-potential leaders as a separate segment, even though they struggled with the concept for many years. This concept can be extended to other roles as well. Certainly HR needs to approach segmentation thoughtfully and cautiously, but it is really a matter of continuing to educate people to expect differences based on ROIP rather than to expect sameness. An airline whose managers have been trained in segmentation thinking will not interpret special incentives for flight attendants as a sign that flight attendants are favored over pilots. At such an airline, the managers would understand those incentives as a natural consequence of the particular organizational role of flight attendants.

The trick to making segmentation work is the use of *logic-driven analysis* (to identify the limited areas in which a different deal really would make a difference), *leadership support* (to instill the recognition that workforce segmentation is essential to the execution of the business strategy in much the same way that customer segmentation is essential), and *transparency* (to communicate clearly and thoughtfully to the entire workforce the why, the what, and the how of segmentation).

The case of CME Group offers a good example of making segmentation work. The process, the tools, and, perhaps most important, the *mind-set* that this organization brought to its segmentation journey are instructive and enlightening. As you read the case, consider how the organization defined the critical skills that would be needed to drive its new growth strategy. Consider as well the role that the company's senior leaders played in designing and championing the new talent strategy, and how they managed the change process with transparency for all.

CME Group: A Focus on Talent Segmentation

Imagine this situation: A company is extremely successful, its initial public offering as the first publicly traded financial exchange performed well beyond expectations, and it is a leader in its industry. What should HR do?

It would be natural to take advantage of good times to upgrade some HR processes or maybe add some programs around onboarding, health, or diversity. Yet CME Group took a different road. CME Group decided that it was time to fundamentally rethink the business strategy, and that meant rethinking talent management.

The operative word in this case is *think*. HR is always thinking, of course. Nothing new is implemented without a lot of problem solving and dialogue. But in CME Group's case, the thinking was unusually deep and thorough; it required recognizing that incenting new business growth demanded new ideas for segmenting and rewarding talent within the organization.

Building on a Tradition of Excellence

As the world's leading and most diverse derivatives marketplace, CME Group was formed through the Chicago Mercantile Exchange's merger with the Chicago Board of Trade in 2007 and the company's acquisition of the New York Mercantile Exchange in 2008. The essence of the business is providing a venue for people to trade financial instruments. Once upon a time that meant a trading pit, but now electronic trading accounts for approximately 80 percent of total volume, and it was in large part the IT prowess of CME Group that drove the company's success. Year after year, CME Group's IT group had driven down transaction costs and increased capability. The CME Globex electronic trading platform was ultrafast and extremely reliable. They had achieved excellence—so what comes next?

The CME Group chief executive officer, Craig Donohue, recognized that the next step was to broaden the company's horizons. CME Group had expanded dramatically within the United States; now it would go global. Furthermore, instead of just matching and clearing futures transactions, future growth would come from providing services to the over-the-counter markets.

CME Group's willingness to reinvent itself belies the common notion that you need a "burning platform" to drive change. CME Group knew they had run their current talent strategy as far it would take them. There was enough vision and cohesion at the top that they were able to logically think about where to go next, and what fundamental organizational changes it would take to get there.

Segmentation Comes from Strategy

It was quite clear that to expand globally and enter the new markets, they would need to hire talent from the outside. Yet HR realized early on that this was not going to be primarily a recruitment exercise. Pursuing these new growth opportunities was going to require a different approach to maximizing the value proposition for both new and existing employees. The key conceptual tool for CME Group was the idea of segmentation. Instead of looking at jobs by level or function, they divided jobs into two segments:

1. Segment 1 (new growth): jobs directly responsible for driving the new growth strategy

2. Segment 2 (core strength): jobs critical to supporting the new growth strategy and running the company

Implicit in this segmentation was the notion that HR approaches and investments would not necessarily be the same across segments. This was a major challenge for CME Group, heretofore an egalitarian culture that had aligned bonus opportunities with job level, regardless of function. Figure 2.3 shows the kind of analysis CME Group undertook to define what a segmented talent strategy might mean to how talent for each segment was sourced, developed, deployed, rewarded, and engaged. This particular figure illustrates the buy-or-build continuum in talent sourcing and how that varied for the two talent segments.

For every key talent-management element—including career paths, pay for individual performance, rewarding what versus rewarding how, and degree of risk in the reward package—they differentiated between what was appropriate for the two segments and how that differed from the current state.

Figure 2.3 Differentiation of Talent Sourcing by Segments

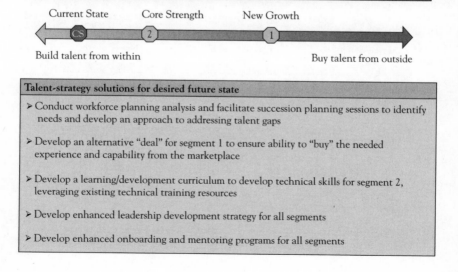

Talent-Sourcing Strategy Continuum

Current State   Core Strength   New Growth

CS   2   1

Build talent from within   Buy talent from outside

Talent-strategy solutions for desired future state

➤ Conduct workforce planning analysis and facilitate succession planning sessions to identify needs and develop an approach to addressing talent gaps

➤ Develop an alternative "deal" for segment 1 to ensure ability to "buy" the needed experience and capability from the marketplace

➤ Develop a learning/development curriculum to develop technical skills for segment 2, leveraging existing technical training resources

➤ Develop enhanced leadership development strategy for all segments

➤ Develop enhanced onboarding and mentoring programs for all segments

Talent Management for Pivotal Jobs

Based on its new growth strategy, CME Group's future success was going to depend increasingly on the individual abilities of some fairly senior dealmakers, business-line and client-relationship managers, and product developers. Where does this kind of talent come from? Do you aim to get the best of the best or simply good performers who can do the job? What sorts of rewards are needed to attract these people and motivate them to succeed?

Once CME Group had identified the jobs with the greatest accountability for strategic growth initiatives, it was clear they needed to motivate employees to achieve very ambitious goals and recruit new world-class talent to help drive results. This meant a reward structure with a big upside—and a downside as well. The logic of this was self-evident, and they found that when they proposed this kind of reward structure, they could attract a different kind of talent than they had in the past. The jobs became appealing to people from investment banking and financial services who were attracted to the reward without being deterred by the risk that goes with it. Figure 2.4 shows the

Figure 2.4 Differentiation of Reward Risks by Segment

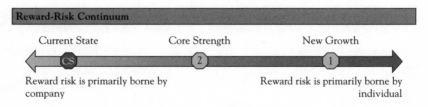

Reward-Risk Continuum		
Current State	Core Strength	New Growth
Reward risk is primarily borne by company		Reward risk is primarily borne by individual

Talent-strategy solutions for desired future state

➤ Directly align individual rewards with individual and team performance and contributions for segment 1 (greater portion of pay is at risk on the basis of individual results)

➤ Tie individual rewards to company and individual performance for segment 2 (greater portion of pay is guaranteed if company achieves goals)

➤ Design pay and performance-management programs to support longer-term career growth for segment 2 (for example, focus on company-oriented incentives, competitive base pay)

same kind of analysis as in Figure 2.3, but this time shows the reward-risk continuum for the two talent segments.

This sort of fundamental change to the way talent was managed also would need to be approved by the board's compensation committee. "We were very much aware that we would need to build the case and put rigor into it so that our compensation committee could understand why we were doing this and the benefits that we expected to achieve," says Hilda Harris Piell, managing director and chief human resources officer.

It was not just that a particular reward package was new. The very idea of segmentation by role was a big change from the past.

"We had a fairly simplistic model in place that had served us well," Piell explains, adding that it had "based incentive opportunities primarily on the employee's level. All employees at the manager level had a certain incentive opportunity, all employees at the associate director level had a certain incentive opportunity, and so on. We didn't differentiate between employees in different roles within the company."

This new idea—that one segment of managerial talent would have a very different reward profile from their peers in another segment—feels odd. Yet it was not so long ago that organizations were uncomfortable with differentiating rewards by performance. This new kind of differentiation is uncommon, but it follows directly from the logic of identifying pivotal roles that drive strategy, and CME Group was willing to let decisions flow from this kind of analysis.

Selling It to the Employees

It is easy to get excited about the new talent strategy, but the whole thing would fall apart if the people most directly affected— the employees—didn't buy into it. Groups that previously had played a key role in driving growth for the company, but were now acting in more of a support capacity, were a key concern. "The hardest part was to get employees to understand that we were not saying 'This person is more valuable than you.' We just wanted to compensate them differently because we wanted their behaviors to be different," said Jamie Parisi, Chief Financial Officer and Managing Director, Finance & Corporate Development.

Likewise, groups that previously had been compensated on a subjective basis would now be required to demonstrate tangible, objective results to justify bonus decisions. "We actually had some people who wanted to know if they could opt out of the higher bonus opportunity. We said, 'Not unless you want to opt out of your job, too.'"

CME Group got all its employees on board by being totally transparent about what was being done and how this was driven by the logic of the business strategy. The fact was that it made sense to everyone to motivate the people with the greatest ability to deliver growth for the company. It was extremely important to emphasize the rigor that was to be applied in assessing the performance of the people in new growth roles. If people in these roles did not achieve their ambitious goals, their compensation would take a hit. However, if they did succeed, then not only would they benefit, but the whole organization would benefit too. More revenue meant greater cash earnings, which meant a larger bonus pool for all.

Lessons Learned at CME Group

Sometimes telling these stories after the fact makes it sound like the organization sat down, logically figured everything out, and rolled out the perfect program. But of course there were bumps along the way, and tweaks were made.

Piell shared an example of a misstep. "There was definitely a lot more work than we anticipated putting the new growth goals in place and measuring them throughout the year," she says. "We did get people much more focused on goals, but the problem was that the process itself became very onerous, with multiple levels of approval. We realized we had swung the pendulum a little too far."

Going in with the mind-set that there was still much to be learned kept everyone, including the compensation committee, open to these sorts of course corrections. The learning mind-set also enhanced buy-in.

"We framed it as a pilot," says Parisi, "with an invitation to everyone to think of themselves as partners in the new talent-management strategy. It gave everyone comfort to know that if elements of this thing didn't work, they could give feedback on what wasn't working and get it fixed."

Overall, CME Group is an outstanding case study of how HR strategy can flow from a thoughtful analysis of the role that different talent segments play in executing a new business strategy and the significant value to be realized through a willingness to invest differentially in those segments.

The One Thing You Should Take Away

Everyone is different, and those differences can reveal how to strike the right compromise between mass customization and rigid standardization. Segmentation requires understanding how people differ in what motivates them and in how they contribute and generate value. The combination of these two perspectives reveals how to customize the employment deal and structure organizational roles to create the highest payoff at the least cost.

3

RISK

Is It Just a Four-Letter Word?

Risk leverage transforms the traditional mind-set that risk is bad. Risk is merely the possibility of a deviation from an expected outcome. As such, risk is something that can be analyzed, planned for, managed, and exploited—leveraged—for the economic benefit of the organization. Taking the right risks is often as vital as avoiding the wrong ones.

Risk is increasingly a major concern of senior leaders and investors. This multifaceted issue encompasses everything from uncertainty in the global economy to variability of interest rates to the unpredictability of individual behavior.

Historically, HR has kept a close eye on some risks, such as the risk of a talent shortfall at the top of the organization or the risks associated with violating laws and regulations. Nevertheless, while other disciplines have well-developed systems for analyzing and optimizing risk, the risks involved in human capital have not yet been addressed so systematically. Most HR units have not yet collaborated on risk management with other functions, such as finance departments and dedicated risk-management departments, whose well-tested frameworks could apply to risk as it is experienced in the HR environment.

This chapter provides some initial frameworks for understanding and managing various types of human capital risk and understanding how HR can effectively leverage risk for sustainable advantage.

A New Mind-Set Around Risk

Although the word *risk* is typically used to represent the chance that something bad will happen, a more precise idea of risk is that it represents unpredictability. Risk is about variability—the chance that something may be higher or lower, bigger or smaller, faster or slower, better or worse than predicted.

Risk is everywhere, and HR professionals continually encounter situations that require decisions to be made about risk. How are those decisions made? Normally, such decisions are a matter of following routines ("We always set incentives this way") or making a gut-level decision ("We would like to promote this person, but he is still unproven and we cannot risk it"). Rarely is human capital risk approached in a systematic, disciplined fashion.

Risk remains a back-burner issue, for the most part. Ask an HR business partner about the HR risks in his unit, and he is unlikely to have a good answer. Ask several HR business partners to create a report on HR risk, and each of them will come back with his or her own way of framing and assessing risk. This is the current state of the profession, but it is also something that we expect to change. HR is increasingly expected to start paying direct attention to risk.

But HR also needs a new mind-set. Having the right mind-set is the first step for HR in dealing intelligently with risk because a sound mind-set brings the right attitude to the issue of risk. Now when HR explicitly identifies a risk, the typical response is to find ways to avoid or reduce it. Yet actuaries and other risk professionals are quite comfortable living with risk; they just make sure that they know which risks to live with, which to prevent, and which to mitigate. They know that there are even times when risk should be encouraged, and they have analysis frameworks to tell them the difference between and among kinds of risks. How can we apply their knowledge and information to HR?

When a new hire works out badly, does this failure indicate that screening needs tightening? Possibly—but HR should not automatically assume that its goal is to minimize the risk of a bad hire. It may be cheaper to accept the risk of an occasional bad hire and then mitigate that risk by weeding out mistakes more quickly.

Typically, however, this trade-off is not explicitly considered. Rather, in order to minimize the risk of a bad hire, HR professionals find someone they are certain can do the job. This is why you find so many recruiters looking for extremely specific backgrounds and skill sets. For example, if an organization needs to replace a logistics analyst for shipments of concrete on the East Coast, then HR's ideal candidate is someone who has done precisely that job before. It is a good strategy for reducing the risk of a bad hire, but restricting the pool of applicants raises costs and increases the time needed to fill the position. A more effective approach might be to take on a less qualified candidate who is immediately available and can grow into the role, or someone who lacks the ideal amount of experience but has exactly the right competencies to grow into a star. This is a case in which HR needs to look at the idea of risk leverage and ask, "Can we gain something by accepting a greater degree of risk?"

The SAS Institute, a consistent winner of "great place to work" rankings, takes an interesting approach to risk in its sick-time policy. This software producer has no specific limits on the sick time an employee can take. There is a risk, of course, that employees will abuse the policy, but SAS leaders asked themselves, "How likely is it that employees will abuse the policy? Even if a few do, what is the magnitude of the cost? How does that compare to the goodwill generated by giving the message that we trust employees and their managers to be responsible about leave?" The company concluded that it made sense to take the risk of having no specific limit on sick leave.

From Mind-Set to Tools and Helpful Frameworks

For HR, acquiring the right mind-set is the first step in dealing intelligently with risk because a sound mind-set brings the right attitude to the issue. The next step is to back up that sound attitude with good tools. Most of the tools and frameworks described in this section are straightforward and will help guide HR through risk issues in a systematic and logical way. Tools and frameworks like these should be in every HR manager's arsenal, both for getting a handle on risk and for communicating about it.

Mapping the Spectrum of HR Risks

A useful way to start is to map the spectrum of HR risks in your organization. There is no standard way to map HR risks, but one approach is to examine the drivers of human capital risk.

Think about where variation occurs in human capital in terms of two factors:

1. How much you spend to generate the human capital "input"

2. How much human capital "output" you ultimately get

Figure 3.1 shows how Towers Watson thinks about the ways in which variation might be determined and predicted with respect to each of these factors of human capital risk. The point here is not to conduct a detailed exploration of every possible element of risk but rather to present a framework that can provide HR with an overview of manageable risks.

Let us first explore the *input* element of human capital risk (represented by the top half of the figure). The input into or investment in the workforce includes what is spent on total rewards. The framework breaks total rewards down into a variable component and a fixed one. The variable component includes bonuses, profit sharing, defined-benefit pensions, and health care costs (in the United States and certain other countries). The fixed component (equity plans, defined-contribution retirement plans, training dollars, work environment, and so on) is characterized by being more stable and thus more predictable, given what is known in advance.

Figure 3.1 Factors in Human Capital Risk

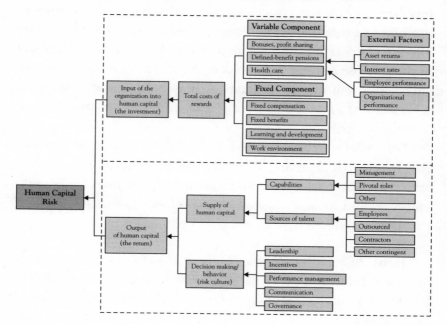

The variable component is affected by external factors, including asset returns and interest rates (which have a major impact on the costs associated with defined-benefit pension plans) and employee and organizational performance (which have a major impact on costs associated with bonuses and profit sharing). Remember, variability is the heart of risk; wherever there is wide variability, there can be unexpected outcomes—good or bad. HR has a responsibility to be aware of issues, such as changes in interest rates, that could affect the total cost of rewards. From the outset, awareness is crucial to risk management.

The *output* element (represented by the bottom half of the figure) is what the organization expects to receive from its investment in its workforce. The Towers Watson framework describes this output in terms of two primary components: (1) the supply of human capital, with respect to its capabilities, and (2) the decision making and behavior in which the workforce actually engages.

The risk component involved in decision making and behavior has been the primary focus of many HR functions, thanks to prominent examples of seemingly well-qualified individuals who have made poor decisions and gotten richly rewarded for them at the expense of their shareholders. Nevertheless, another significant cause of unexpected behavior may be that the systems for selecting and developing talent produce unexpected variations in individual attributes.

Now that we have defined some drivers of various kinds of risk in the HR domain, let us turn to how we might monitor and prioritize those risks and analyze which ones we should embrace and accept as well as those we should mitigate or prevent.

Heat Maps and Traffic Lights Workforce-related risk is all around. Imagine, for example, that your company is in the business of creating animated films. You have a range of critical talent pools, from story writers to animators to producers. There are important parts of your operation in the United States, Canada, South Korea, and France. When your projects have gone off the rails, it has often been because there were too few people in a critical talent pool, or because the quality of the talent was not high enough. A very basic but nevertheless useful tool for tackling this kind of workforce risk is a 3 × 3 matrix of probability versus impact—or, in the case of Figure 3.2, two matrices, one for risks related to the quantity of talent and one for risks related to the quality of talent.

When the various risks are plotted on this kind of heat map, it is evident which risks will offer pivotal value if their impact or likelihood is reduced, which risks can probably be tolerated, and which ones need further study. In this case, the notable risks are not having enough animators (left-hand side of the heat map) and not having high-performing producers (right-hand side of the heat map). The maps help HR think through where the risks are in a systematic way.

Figure 3.2 Heat Maps Showing Risk in Terms of Quantity and Quality of Talent

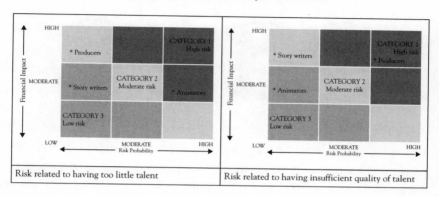

An organization expanding rapidly in Russia might plot its jobs on these heat maps. If the product is simple, there may be some jobs (for instance, in sales) where there is a high risk of not having enough reps, and the financial impact of that short-fall would be great. In a job such as government relations, the risk might not be in quantity (the jobs can easily be filled), but in quality, and a few excellent people may mean the difference between success and failure for the enterprise.

A well-known rubric is that the human mind can hold only seven things, plus or minus two, in short-term memory. That is why this kind of tool is so useful—it allows us to look at many jobs or HR practices at once and pick out the ones we need to focus on. (An example using a similar framework for decisions about incentive risk is included in the case study of PNC Bank at the end of this chapter.)

Heat maps are a useful tool, but sometimes stakeholders want a simpler presentation of the data. A presentation using a graphic of a traffic light simply identifies an issue as red (meaning that there is trouble), yellow (meaning that there is a possible concern), or green (meaning that the situation surrounding the issue is good). Although this approach does not give answers different from those provided by a heat map, it is prudent to

Figure 3.3 Traffic Light to Highlight Risk of Talent Shortfalls

Finance   HR   Marketing   Production

consider what sort of data presentation will be most effective in communicating with stakeholders. Figure 3.3 shows data presentation using a graphic of a traffic light.

Inverse Heat Maps Heat maps offer a good way to systematically identify risks, but from our point of view they have one problem—they focus on risk reduction, not risk leverage. Most people looking at a heat map will immediately want to eliminate risks falling into "Category 1": the top right area of the map, which is traditionally colored in red. What the usual heat maps miss are risks that offer an upside. Here are some areas in HR where the upside of risk may be more important than the downside:

- Building a capability that will not be used at all if certain future conditions do not occur, but that may be useful if those conditions do occur

- Hiring more people than are needed at the moment, an action that will certainly increase costs but may prove strategically valuable if the market grows faster than expected and if talent is in short supply

- Hiring individuals who are atypical and who may fail because they don't "fit in," but who also, precisely because of that quality, may produce breakthrough innovations

Sutton (2002) argues that hiring "weirdos" is a good idea. Think of it as hiring someone who will say, "We should turn left" when everyone else is saying, "Turn right." The advantage of having a few weirdos around is that they broaden the talent portfolio and may make you ready for a future that really *does* require turning left—even though that is a less likely future. Hiring them entails a cost but also creates an upside to risk because the weirdos may offer ideas that would not otherwise be available in the talent portfolio.

In any of these situations, it is helpful if HR looks at the upside of risk with the same rigor brought to bear on the downside of risk. Recall the heat map pictured in Figure 3.2, where the y-axis label "Financial Impact" indicates the downside of risk. An easy way to look at the upside of risk is to produce an inverse heat map by using the label "Magnitude of Positive Financial Impact" on the heat map's y-axis (see Figure 3.4).

The point of the inverse heat map is to highlight opportunities that might be discarded out-of-hand because they are a gamble. If something is very unlikely (the left-hand side of the heat map), it is not worth pursuing, but opportunities that are somewhat unlikely but would have a high payoff are attractive (top right portion of the heat map).

The value of an inverse heat map is that it gives HR a way to think through and explain decisions involving the *likelihood* of a *negative* outcome (the new capability will never be used, the extra staff will not be needed, the risky hire will not work out),

Figure 3.4 Inverse Heat Map Showing Opportunities

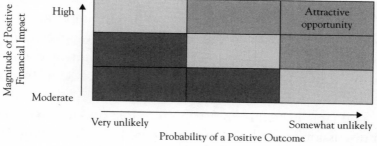

but with the *possibility* of a *positive* outcome, one that makes the risk worth taking.

Tolerance Analysis for Performance Variance

In engineering, there is a well-known principle regarding variability. This is the principle known as *tolerance*, and it can teach us to consider risk in a different way. In engineering, *tolerance* refers to the allowable deviation from or variation within a standard; and *tolerance analysis* is the engineering activity that assesses the implications of such deviations or variations. When it comes to human resources, the engineering idea of tolerance analysis can be applied to employee performance, something we will call *performance tolerance analysis*. The idea is to understand the implications of deviations from performance standards, and adjust the tolerance for such deviations accordingly. For example, how much variation can there be in the performance of a mechanical part? In a flat-screen TV monitor, the brightness of each pixel has to fit within a low range of tolerance for variation because an overly bright or dark pixel would stand out. At the same time, the buttons on the remote control device do not have to be uniformly yielding or resistant to the touch. The responsiveness of the buttons can fit within a higher range of tolerance for variation. Therefore, the TV manufacturer will put a lot more effort into the pixels than into the buttons on the remote.

So the tightness of performance around a standard is part of tolerance analysis. It can also consider how the *value* of positive and negative deviations can have different implications. For example, if the pixels on the screen last much longer than the standard tolerance, that is not a problem (it might even be a positive feature), but if they burn out in much shorter time than the standard, that is a problem.

The same principle applies both to jobs and to tasks. Recall our discussion of a pilot's job as compared to a flight attendant's job (see Chapter Two). The job of a pilot is obviously an essential operational job, with significant responsibility for passengers' safety. The performance curves and the high minimum standards set for all pilots point to low tolerance for variation from a level of performance that meets those standards. For flight attendants, by contrast, the tolerance for variations in performance need not be so low, and the cost of a flight attendant's poor performance is far less than it would be if a pilot performed poorly. The job of a flight attendant also entails more room for an upside in terms of provision of excellent service. Figure 3.5 can help us think clearly about the concept of tolerance for variation from standards with respect to jobs and tasks.

It is worth noting, however, that even though there is a lower overall cost associated with performance variation in a flight attendant's job, we might not want to see performance variation in all aspects of that job. This idea becomes clearer if we think in terms of tasks rather than jobs. All airlines need to keep variations in performance tightly controlled when it comes to those tasks of a flight attendant that are related to safety, but when it comes to tasks involving customer service, the best degree of variance is open to debate.

Consider the examples of Southwest Airlines and of WestJet, a small Canadian airline based in Calgary, Alberta. Both airlines

Figure 3.5 Performance Tolerance Analysis for Two Airline Jobs

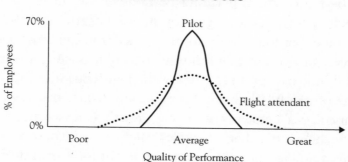

actively encourage variance in the performance of customer-facing tasks. Onboard announcements cover the essential messages but are not canned; they reflect the cabin crew's personalities and lightness of mood. This kind of variance is in keeping with the personality of each organization and further reinforces the "fun" factor that plays a central role in each airline's customer proposition and strategy.

HR, in using the principle of tolerance for variations in job performance, must ask several fundamental questions: *Where do we need to invest to keep variation in performance tightly controlled? Where is it all right to leave the standards for variation somewhat looser? And where do we want to encourage a range of behavior because we want variation?* With these questions addressed, HR can choose the interventions that best enable the desired outcomes. A good place to start is to ask whether there are jobs where the organization may be missing out on the upside of risk because tolerances for variation in performance are too tight.

Portfolio Theory and Risk Diversification

In investing, an important framework for managing risk is offered by portfolio theory, that is, the idea that if you have the right mix of investment assets (stocks, bonds, annuities, and so forth), you are in less danger if any one of them goes down because, overall, the ups and downs balance out. Might a similar framework be useful to HR?

The most natural place for portfolio theory in HR is where there is a significant degree of future uncertainty. Boudreau (2010) uses portfolio theory to show when it would be a good idea to invest in two possible future scenarios at once (for example, by building two groups, each with qualifications well suited to one of two highly likely future situations). If the most likely scenario for a company is strong growth in Asia and weaker growth in Europe, then efficiency might suggest putting all the organization's resources into sourcing talent for Asia. But if there is a reasonable chance that the company's European operations will grow faster than they are growing today, then devoting all the organization's resources to the more likely scenario (growth in Asia) would be like putting all its eggs in one basket. Financial advisors have long known that we should spread our investments between stocks and bonds, even if we suspect that stocks will outperform bonds. Portfolio theory shows the value of spreading one's bets, and it even provides formulas showing how to do it (for details, see Boudreau, 2010). In this case, spreading the organization's bets might mean pushing some investment toward sourcing capability in Europe along with investing in Asia. Yes, it is possible that all the company's growth will occur in Asia (just as all our assets' growth might occur in stocks rather than in bonds), in which case the company will not use all the talent it built for Europe. But if growth does turn out to occur in Europe, the organization's investment will protect it from being caught without any ready talent.

Similarly, HR might come under pressure to reduce the cost of campus recruiting. One strategy would be to cut the number of universities back to just the top few. But the principle of risk diversification would caution against that. There is value in having a portfolio of universities with which the organization maintains relationships, even at some additional cost, because it reduces risk. In some future situations, the organization may be able to successfully fill its vacancies from the top universities without using its relationships with other schools. But if it turns out that the future presents tough competition for candidates from those top schools, or if the organization's demand exceeds the supply from those schools, the company will be glad to have invested in relationships with universities beyond the top tier.

More generally, HR seldom should assume that investing only for the most probable future is an acceptable route. HR needs to plan for that future while also considering possibilities for hedging its bets. Risk diversification and portfolio theory are bread-and-butter issues for the CEO, and if HR makes (and explains) its decisions with these frameworks, then HR will get better support from the top.

Experimentation

Another tool in the arsenal of risk-savvy HR leaders is experimentation. If it proves difficult to attract candidates for factory jobs in Malaysia, someone might suggest that instead of job ads being placed only in the "manufacturing jobs" sections of newspapers and posted on Web employment sites, they be put up at bus stops as well. Too often, HR shies away from such unproven ideas on the grounds that they would be likely to attract few or no viable applicants, and that the money saved by forgoing the strategy would be a certainty. That analysis is correct, but it comes from the risk-avoidance mentality. A more sophisticated view of risk is that there is a wide range of possible outcomes, including good outcomes—even though informed opinion would say that a particular experiment will not work. At that point, it becomes clear that experimentation is a useful risk-management tool. Trying out tactics at a low cost keeps the risk low, too, and creates the possibility of an upside.

It is probably not so much that HR departments do not understand the value of this kind of experimentation as that they are not good at explaining it. If an HR department conducts an experiment that fails, too often HR and its constituents interpret this event as HR's having done something wrong. If HR learns to frame experiments in terms of leveraging risk, then it will be easier to conduct them without suffering a penalty if an experiment returns a less than positive result. Think of an experiment as HR's equivalent of buying an option. The cost of an option is typically a fraction of the underlying asset price, and the riskier the option (that is, the more it is "out of the money"), the lower the price. As Boudreau (2010) points out, this is precisely how disciplines such as R&D, product development, and consumer marketing successfully balance risk and return. The key is to apply the same mind-set to HR.

Data-Based Simulations

In most cases, HR can manage risk by looking at the issues systematically and applying a few simple, logical frameworks to guide decision making. There are a number of analytical tools, however, that are important in helping HR forecast risks. Many of these tools are already in use within specific HR disciplines.

Take the example of stochastic forecasts, which are routinely used to predict the future impact that potential changes in interest rates and in rates of return on assets will have on pension values. Stochastic forecasts use Monte Carlo simulations to forecast a range of possible future outcomes over a multiyear period. This kind of analysis is familiar to and routinely used by benefits departments to predict the possible future cost of total rewards under a range of scenarios.

Figure 3.6 illustrates the application of stochastic forecasts to a company's total rewards portfolio (salaries, pensions, health care benefits, incentive compensation, equity plans, recognition, training, learning and development, profit sharing, and so on). The organization created a stochastic forecast for its current portfolio of total rewards and compared the variability in cost of that portfolio over a multiyear period against that of an alternative total rewards portfolio. What interests us from a risk perspective is the size of each bar. There is not a great difference in expected cost between the two alternatives, but the current program is more variable (that is, it has more risk). If we look at the last year shown in the figure, we see that the current program could cost from as little as $1 billion to as much as $1.4 billion, whereas the alternative varies from $1.1 billion to $1.3 billion. This does not necessarily mean that the alternative program is better. In order to make a sound decision, however, it

Figure 3.6 A Stochastic Forecast

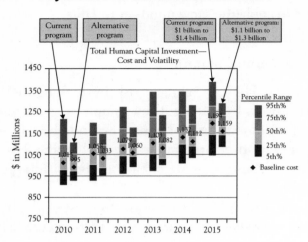

is important to know the risk, which is what this tool helps HR to do. Whenever HR is interested in forecasting the future of a quantitative element, this kind of analysis can show the spread of possible outcomes over time.

Risk Posture

A final useful framework helps HR be explicit in identifying the organization's posture toward various risks. The four possible postures are as follows:

1. *Accept:* The impact and probability are low enough that no action is required.
2. *Prevent:* The risk is a real concern, and action is taken to prevent it.
3. *Mitigate:* It is impractical or unnecessary to try to eliminate the risk, but steps can be taken to mitigate it.
4. *Embrace:* The risk has a potential upside and should be embraced.

For example, consider these postures toward the risk of turn-over in a key position:

Risk Posture	Action
Accept	If a loss occurs, we will react, but it is a risk we accept.
Prevent	We will introduce retention measures, such as long-term incentives.
Mitigate	We will ensure that there is a succession-management plan with short- and intermediate-term successors.
Embrace	Losing a person in a key role has a cost, and there is a risk that we will not find an equally good replacement, but it is also an opportunity to refresh the team and bring in new ideas. On the basis of our knowledge of candidates in the market, the upside potential is great enough that this is a risk we should be happy to embrace. In fact, it may be that turnover is too low to capture this upside of risk, and that HR should introduce measures to reduce retention.

For all the tools and frameworks we have outlined here, the goals for HR are, first, to think clearly about risk and, second, to recognize that not all risks need to be minimized. With risk becoming a much bigger issue, HR will be expected to be able to make good risk decisions and then explain those decisions in ways that are easy for stakeholders to understand. A few tools, such as stochastic forecasting, require specialized skills, but for the most part HR leaders do not need any special training to tackle risk in a more professional way.

As can be seen, just about every HR decision lends itself to the mind-set and thought process that surround risk lever-age. The consistent and rigorous application of the tools and frameworks we have discussed here can help transform how HR thinks about risk. Instead of viewing risk as a factor to be consis-tently mitigated or avoided, HR can look at risk as another key variable in the quest to drive evidence-based change.

Nowhere is this mind-set of risk leverage more present than at PNC Bank. The following case study illustrates the organization's quest to truly understand the behavioral risk implicit in its incentive compensation plans. Through the use of the frameworks and tools we have discussed here, not only did PNC squarely address and leverage this particular risk, it developed an overall process and framework that it can now apply to all types of HR risk.

PNC Bank: Creating Risk Leverage

Whom do human resource professionals regularly work with outside their own function? The answer may typically include top management, finance, line managers, employees in general, and perhaps union leaders. Yet the most recent addition to the list might be risk-management professionals. PNC, a large commercial bank headquartered in Pittsburgh, PA, has pioneered an analytical approach to linking financial performance, compensation, and risk management. Their approach demonstrates the value HR can bring to complex business problems by partnering with various stakeholders, including risk management.

No industry is more focused on the management of risk than financial services. Primarily involved in borrowing and lending funds and other transactions in financial instruments, banks and other financial institutions are constantly in the business of managing risk. Every decision requires an evaluation of risk and return; therefore, these companies must develop an effective enterprise risk-management framework and risk-management culture so that risks, including HR risks, are managed to benefit shareholders.

The financial crisis of 2007 demonstrated the devastating effects of poorly managed risk on investors, institutions, consumers, and the overall economy. Triggered by a liquidity shortfall in the banking system, this crisis caused the collapse of large financial institutions and, in some cases, required significant government intervention. Many economists consider it the worst financial crisis since the Great Depression.

Nevertheless, throughout the financial meltdown, PNC weathered the storm remarkably well. The company consistently outperformed its peers throughout the cycle, doubled in size, and is now the sixth largest bank in the United States by deposits. Further, PNC was named Bank of the Year in the U.S.A. by *The Banker* magazine.

Like many financial services industry companies, PNC operates in a highly competitive environment, with more than 50,000 employees serving a diverse range of clients and communities. Unlike some others, however, PNC was serious about risk management well before the financial crisis, and its skill in managing various risks enabled the company to go through the financial crisis relatively unscathed.

Still, PNC does not view risk management as a separate task but as a way of doing business. In fact, risk management is embedded in PNC's culture. During town hall meetings with employees, in management updates to senior leaders, and in presentations to the board of directors, the CEO often starts with PNC's PowerLink symbol (Figure 3.7). This image portrays PNC's belief that risk management, customer satisfaction, and growth

Figure 3.7 PNC's PowerLink Symbol

are linked. PNC Chairman and Chief Executive Officer James E. Rohr believes and reinforces the principle that risk management is "everyone's business." The commitment to a moderate risk profile is closely incorporated in the company's HR practices and compensation programs.

Incentive Plans and Risk

PNC's commitment to risk management influenced key decisions during the acquisition of National City. As part of that acquisition, PNC inherited hundreds of incentive plans, many of them with complicated design features and some reflecting a different compensation philosophy than PNC's. Not only did administering these incentive plans create an enormous administrative challenge, it also presented significant risks to the organization. HR needed to develop a thoughtful process to evaluate these plan designs using objective assessment criteria that would enable business leaders and HR to make informed decisions quickly.

This was the beginning of a journey, still far from over, during which HR partnered with the business, finance, and risk professionals to bring a new sophistication to how HR understands and manages risk. Although the issue at hand was the risk associated with incentive plans, it was clear that by applying a rigorous analytical approach, PNC could establish a model to be used across the HR function.

Over the past two decades, compensation professionals have developed sophisticated analytical approaches for incentive plan designs. Generally, plans are tested through the lens of business needs with answers to questions such as:

- What performance and behavior should the plans incent?
- Are the incentives aligned with shareholder value creation?

- Do these support the business's strategic priorities?
- Do the plans provide competitive incentive opportunities that will attract, motivate, and retain the desired talent?

However, this framework does not explicitly take risk into consideration. A growing emphasis on pay and risk has emerged following the recent financial meltdown. Companies, shareholders, and regulators became more aware of the need to align compensation with sound risk management and long-term value creation. PNC was very clear that the assessment framework it was developing would have to provide clarity on both dimensions.

A Risk-Based Incentive Plan Assessment

PNC tackled the need to develop a risk-based incentive plan assessment by forming a close partnership between the compensation professionals, finance, business leaders, and the risk-management team. All four stakeholders had to be engaged for PNC to make sound judgments on incentives. Together they developed a four-step process for the evaluation:

1. Conduct plan inventory
2. Evaluate plan design and governance risks
3. Assess the potential for earnings
4. Provide recommended action steps

Through the inventory process, all legacy incentive plans were documented to provide clarity on plan basics, such as participants, payout frequency, type of metrics, the determination process, and historical payout. This foundational information, albeit very basic, provided an enormous amount of insight early in the process. With that information in hand, business and HR leaders quickly made the decision to eliminate more than one hundred incentive plans and migrated the participants to similarly structured PNC plans.

The next step was to evaluate the operational aspects of the remaining plans and their financial impact on PNC. This analysis considered the following questions:

- Does the plan incorporate balanced metrics and multiple measures? That is, does the plan avoid an overreliance on a single measure that might not fully reflect the business results?
- Are the metrics based on individual, team, or corporate performance? Metrics based on individual performance can create a higher level of risk for the organization.
- Are the metrics based on top-line or bottom-line measures? Undue emphasis on top-line measures can generate problems.
- What is the nature of the payout curves? Are they steep? Are there cliffs? Are payoffs uncapped? All these features impact how an individual will behave.
- Is there management discretion in the amount awarded? Management discretion can act as a brake on risky behavior.

The second set of criteria targeted business-specific questions:

- Does the plan cover individuals or functions that take principal risk and/or commit capital?
- What is the level of residual risk?
- How well collateralized is the principal risk or commitment to capital?
- Is the business primarily, or exclusively, fee-based or advisory?

Any plans that engendered a degree of risk inconsistent with PNC's risk appetite were retired immediately. The remaining

Figure 3.8 Risk-Probability Matrix

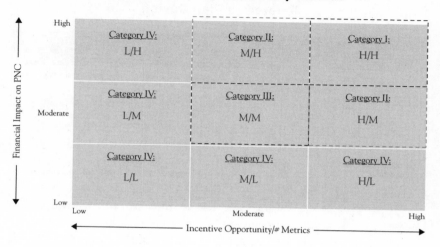

plans were evaluated with the use of a simple 3 × 3 matrix of incentive opportunities versus the financial impact (in aggregate). See Figure 3.8.

After identifying plans with a higher probability to create risks, PNC took the analysis to the next level by assessing how risk could be mitigated through effective management and plan governance processes. Here, HR's relationship with the risk function proved crucial to classifying governance categories that could mitigate plan design risks (Figure 3.9). After this analysis, the risk-management function determined which of the high-risk plans needed to be redesigned or retired (Figure 3.10). At this point, the HR, business, finance, and risk teams had documented a clear understanding of the risks associated with the incentive plans. Their methodical process and intuitive frameworks made it easy to explain their rationale to other stakeholders.

Once the assessment process was complete, the path to implementation also became clearer. In partnership with business leaders, the HR team launched the communication effort. In addition to informing employees about what incentive plans would change and how, they also focused on the "why," thus

Figure 3.9 Mitigating Factors in Reducing Risks Related to Plan Design

Risk Mitigation Category	Representative Mitigating Factors
Role Design	■ Roles work in concert with one another, and therefore individuals cannot take risky actions independently
	■ Clear separation of operation and production/origination roles through Centralized Operations Group (Separation of roles limits production/origination role's ability to directly influence underwriting, funding, and processing decisions)
Pay Determination Methodology	■ Allocation of pool to individuals is discretionary
	■ Incentive payouts for transactions with credit risk rating downgrades, charge-offs within 12 months, and loans paid off within 12 months are considered unearned advances against future incentive earnings (clawback)
Performance Measures	■ Incentives based on profitability measure (free cash flow) incorporate risk adjustments based on several factors, such as risk rating, probability of default, etc.
	■ In addition to financial metrics, performance against strategic goals is a key qualitative factor
Pay Mix	■ Long-term incentives, including time-based stock awards and performance-based LTI grants, represent a significant portion of total compensation
	■ Modest short-term incentive payouts for most incumbents
Governance	■ Compensation Committee of the Board reviews and approves the bonus pool as well as key individual decisions, and/or multiple levels of sign-offs are required

providing employees with a better understanding of PNC's risk-management decision making.

"Typically, we would spend a lot of time and energy on the *what* but not enough time on the *why*," says Bei Ling, PNC Senior Vice President of Total Rewards. "In this process, we learned that if employees understand and relate to the rationale for change, it is easier for them to accept it, even if the change negatively impacts them."

Design Versus Governance

PNC recognized that the risk in incentive plans is not just a matter of design. Governance is equally if not more important. Effective risk management is about a sound understanding of the risks taken and about an effective governance process to evaluate, monitor, and mitigate those risks. Effective corporate

Figure 3.10 Final Assessment of Actual Plan Risk

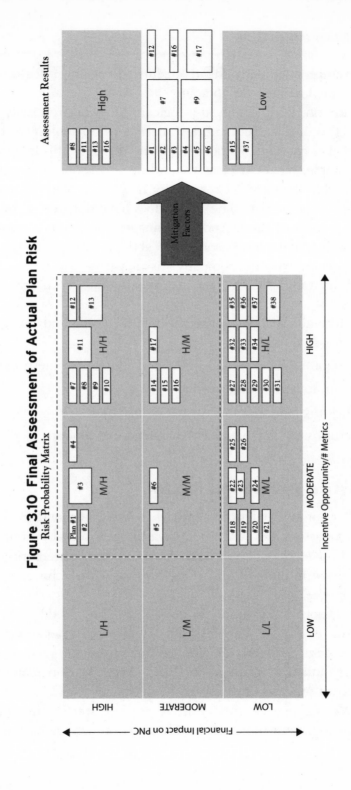

governance maximizes the risk-adjusted return and minimizes the residual risk for the company.

Early on, PNC deployed a logical framework to clarify decision rights and accountabilities, such as who should give input, who makes recommendations, and who decides. This framework, for example, makes it clear that while a risk officer would not decide what incentive plan to use or how much plan participants should be compensated, he or she does have to agree to the plan before it is put in place. And risk managers play an important role in ensuring that plan participants' actions throughout the year are consistent with the company's risk appetite.

Ultimately, PNC's governance process aims to ensure:

- A formalized and consistently applied design and approval process
- A rigorous exception, dispute, and adjustment methodology
- Accurate and timely payouts
- Ongoing plan monitoring and oversight
- Scrutiny when payouts are over a certain amount

Analytical Frameworks and HR

PNC's rigorous analytical approach to assessing and managing the risks associated with incentive plans is based on our concept of *risk leverage*. This means distinguishing between risks that need to be minimized and risks that are within the company's risk appetite.

A lesson to be more widely applied has to do with how HR can leverage the analytical know-how of other disciplines. In this case, by working with risk-management professionals, finance, and the business, the PNC compensation team made significant progress on a sensitive and difficult topic.

"We realize that this effort is just the start of integrating risk management more effectively into compensation programs and policies," said Ling. "At the time it was initiated, I wasn't aware of an existing practice in the marketplace. I am encouraged by the outcome and possibilities. Sound risk management must support PNC's relentless focus on shareholder value creation and business growth momentum. The challenge ahead of us, and all companies, is to identify and build the infrastructure to track the appropriate risk-based metrics that balance the risk and return so that they can be incorporated into day-to-day business decisions and incentive plans. The metrics have to be intuitive and easily understood by employees—this is not an easy task."

The risk-management group's involvement in incentive compensation was not a one-time project. It has become an integral part of PNC's incentive compensation design and governance process. Along with business leaders, finance, HR, and legal, the risk-management group is a critical part of the team in making incentive plan design decisions.

"We expect that great progress will continue to be made in the next few years," said PNC's Joan Gulley, EVP and Chief Human Resources Officer. "We've come a long way and can see the areas where we need to learn more."

This case demonstrates how HR at PNC has fully embraced risk as an element that can be squarely faced and successfully managed. In addition to deepening the understanding of inherent risks in business decisions, PNC is also exploring opportunities to further leverage risk management into other HR programs and practices more effectively. For example, most recently, PNC enhanced the performance management process under which risk management discipline would be formally integrated as a key element, in addition to business results and other demonstrated behaviors. This enhancement will not only help facilitate compensation decisions and the talent-management process, it will also raise more awareness throughout the organization about the importance of risk management.

This rigorous and formal approach to risk management is new for most HR professionals, but, following PNC's model, it is destined to be a core competency going forward.

The One Thing You Should Take Away

It's easy to react to risk by trying to avoid it or reduce it, but the most effective approach is to understand risk as both a potential danger and a potential opportunity. This often means going against the traditional HR position of mitigating risk and approaching human capital more like an investment portfolio. Approaching risk as something to be leveraged, rather than only avoided, is the way to find the "smart bets" that hold significant returns.

4

YOUR HR PORTFOLIO

Is It Less Than the Sum of Its Parts?

The principle of *integration and synergy* is about understanding how different HR solutions mesh with one another and with other organizational processes to deliver a unique and distinctly compelling proposition to the organization and the workforce. It is about ensuring that decisions work together in concert and reinforce each other such that $1 + 1 = 3$.

Integration means ensuring that HR programs are aligned so that they do not work at cross-purposes. When integration is handled well, HR programs reinforce one another to achieve synergies so that the whole is more than the sum of its parts.

For HR, integration can be the source of breakthroughs or frustration. On the breakthrough side, there are the talent and leadership development systems of organizations like GE that seem at first glance to merely be collections of world-class elements. For example, their forced-distribution performance system identifies the top and bottom performers, weeds out the bottom performers, and replaces them with superior talent. This type of system differentiates between performance levels in a way that is well understood and that guides winning behaviors. Another world-class element, GE's development system, provides excellent learning experiences and well-crafted career paths that produce just the sort of leaders most needed for growth. The GE HR system has led to outstanding results that understandably impress employees, leaders, shareholders, and peer organizations. But even though the individual elements of such a program may be laudable in themselves, the breakthrough comes in how those elements work together (integration) and how they combine to create a result far better than what any one of them could have produced alone (synergy).

On the frustration side, we need only consider how an organization may learn about the need for integration the hard way, by implementing only one element of GE's system. Perhaps the most frequently copied element is GE's forced-distribution performance-management approach. They expect this will provide a basis for recognizing the best and weeding out the worst. However, as many organizations have learned to their dismay, emulating only one element of a successful system does not produce breakthrough results and can actually have significant adverse consequences.

Imposing a forced-distribution system is more likely to produce worse outcomes than without it, if it is implemented without GE's diverse global business portfolio to provide recognition and development, or GE's decades-long culture of frank and honest performance discussions, or GE's world-class executive development, or GE's employment brand that allows GE to find great candidates to replace employees who leave.

Thus lack of synergy and integration creates frustration—individual elements of a system may work well in isolation but may not "add up" with other elements unless they are all combined in a specific way to support and integrate with the overall talent and leadership development systems. This is one reason for a familiar paradox: HR leaders are lauded for world-class processes in individual HR areas, but their constituents just do not seem to appreciate the value of all this good work. The answer may be to step back and consider how to make individual HR elements work better *together* rather than strive to bring them all individually to a world-class level.

Integration and Synergy Within the HR Function

The first level of the principle of integration and synergy exists within the HR function, and the focus is on how the elements of HR can work together. The easiest way to recognize integration is to look for where it is missing. For example, if an organization provides outstanding training in customer service to one hundred people just before laying off fifty of them, then clearly that was not a good investment. If recruiting goes to great lengths to source and select individual high achievers while the performance-management system is rewarding teamwork, then there will be higher turnover and poor performance. If the reward system pays well above the market average to attract top performers, that money will be wasted if recruiting minimizes cost-of-hire and time-to-fill by cutting corners on selection and onboarding in such a way that average performers are brought in.

A famous case of negative synergy occurred when Starbucks introduced a program to reduce theft by employees. The coffee-house chain decided to remove the pockets from baristas' aprons, which could make it all too easy for a barista to pocket a few dollars that should have gone into the till. We can readily imagine the argument that was made for this program, and how reasonable it sounded. Unfortunately, however, this effort was completely at odds with the Starbucks employment brand, which emphasized treating baristas as valued talent. The theft-reduction program was fine, and the employment brand was fine, but together they were in conflict, and the net result was negative synergy. Starbucks, realizing that its employment brand mattered more than any potential loss due to theft, reinstated the pockets. It is important to recognize that the same theft-reduction program might make sense in a different company with a different employment brand. The issue is not that it was a dumb idea but that it was at odds with an important part of Starbucks' HR strategy.

Another example of lack of synergy can be seen in professional services firms. In most consulting firms, consultants' performance appraisals are based on an annual review by their boss. This may seem completely uncontroversial; if you look at the job design, however, you will see that consulting work is based on client engagements, not on an annual cycle. Furthermore, the design of the organization calls for the consultant to report to the project leader for the duration of a particular client engagement, and so the boss responsible for the annual appraisal does not direct or observe the consultant's day-to-day work. In the absence of some sort of review after each engagement, the performance appraisal feels disconnected from the consultant's work. Here, again, there is nothing wrong with annual appraisals, and there is nothing wrong with designing work around client engagements, but if the work design and the appraisal system are not integrated, they end up creating negative synergy.

HR leaders can do a number of things to promote synergy and integration. One is to avoid encouraging the out-of-context creation of world-class training programs, sourcing projects, or diversity initiatives. The more savvy HR leader will encourage programs that synergize with everything else HR is doing. If an enthusiastic but narrowly focused program designer created an award-winning mentorship program, how would an organization that values synergy receive it? If the mentorship program did not sync well with the organization's management development process, the program would get a thumbs-down. The individual excellence of a program is not as important as what it adds to or subtracts from the total equation. Clearly, careful analysis and communication are needed to keep program designers motivated but also synergistic.

A useful way for an HR leader to examine integration and synergy in the HR function is to array the functional elements of the talent life cycle (attract, select, orient, develop, deploy, assess, reward, and so on) and ask, "Do these separate elements of our deliverables work well together?" One can imagine mapping combinations of these elements against ratings of how well they work individually and how well they integrate (or how much they fail to integrate) with each other function. Examining how different HR functions work together and communicate is another way to approach HR integration.

Synergy is not just a nice-sounding concept; it can be measured. For example, a study by Towers Watson showed a wide range of talent-management programs that were significantly more effective when they were linked to a globally consistent, broad-based job-leveling architecture (Figure 4.1). Leveling is worthwhile on its own, but synergistic effects show up when many elements of talent management are linked to it.

There is an even higher plane of thinking that we sometimes see when an HR leader promotes universal themes that keep everyone in HR, and even beyond HR, pointed in the same direction. For example, in an organization that values diversity, someone designing a coaching program will not need to be directed to ensure that his or her work dovetails with the organizational focus on diversity. That focus will naturally be a

Figure 4.1 Job-Leveling Framework

Globally consistent job-leveling systems provide a framework and starting point for integration and synergy of multiple talent-management programs.

Percentage of organizations reporting their talent management programs are very effective

Program	Have globally consistent broad-based job leveling*	Do not have globally consistent broad-based job leveling	Difference
Leadership assessment	34%	15%	19%
Leadership development	31%	18%	13%
Competency models/architecture	23%	9%	14%
Employee learning and development	36%	21%	15%
Workforce planning	20%	11%	9%
Talent movement/rotations	18%	10%	8%
Critical-role identification	30%	16%	14%
Performance management	37%	25%	12%

*Numbers represent percentage of multinational respondents who report their program being very effective.

design consideration because the theme of diversity has been so deeply woven into the HR mind-set.

Integration and Synergy Between HR and Other Organizational Units

The principle of integration and synergy also offers insights into how HR can enhance its contributions through its relationships with the businesses it supports as well as with other functions. There are at least three ways HR can improve its integration with other units: by allocating its investments on the basis of those units' priorities, by linking HR measures to business measures, and by using the logical frameworks developed by other functions.

HR can integrate its efforts with the strategic needs of business units by fully understanding talent segmentation and then optimizing talent investments. Although HR may be dutifully pursuing such goals as building world-class competencies for a business unit, if the biggest improvement in that unit's performance will come from more rapid filling of vacancies, then the HR organization should support faster recruitment. Imagine the frustration the unit head feels as she tries to grow the business but is stymied by lack of staff—and all the while HR, although busy doing great work, is doing work that does not address the unit head's immediate needs. Her drive to grow in the short term is not wrong, and neither are HR's efforts to work on competencies for the long term, but HR and the business unit are not integrating their efforts.

Synergy develops when great programs are delivered by HR and combined with insight and priorities that are based on business units' needs. Either of these two elements alone would be a strong contribution, but together they can lead to an outcome greater than the delivery of high-quality but out-of-context HR programs. Davenport and Harding (2010) share the example of how United Airlines cleverly made employee recognition a key element of its managers' jobs and enabled them by providing each manager with a recognition toolkit that included ideas and rewards associated with each of the organization's five performance imperatives. This is an example of creating synergy among an HR program (in this case, employee recognition), organizational strategy, and the critical role of frontline managers. We also saw this in the case of CME Group (Chapter Two), where quite different reward programs were designed for different parts of the business on the basis of HR's insights into what the different units needed. Another means of integrating the work of HR with the businesses it supports is to find a link between HR measures and measures that the business units care about; this idea is discussed later in this book, in the case of the Royal Bank of Scotland (RBS) Group (see Chapter Eleven).

Synergy from HR's work with other functions also comes about when HR uses logical and analytical frameworks from those functions to organize and understand the value of HR; for an example of this kind of synergy in action, see the case of the Royal Bank of Canada (RBC) (Chapter Six). Again, the key is $1 + 1 = 3$: great HR combined with other functions' logic and analytics add up to the chance for breakthrough results.

Integration and Synergy Between Organizational Units

A final, often overlooked domain of integration and synergy exists between and among organizational units themselves. Some leadership development programs rely on moving leaders between business units. This means that units will need to sacrifice some of their best performers so that those performers can gain needed development elsewhere. It also means that units must be willing to move leaders out in order to create vacancies for incoming talent. In an organization with a diversity of business units and a culture that regards leaders as corporate rather than unit-specific resources, opportunities can be created that otherwise would not exist because the synergy of integrated units creates something greater than individual units could accomplish on their own.

What can be overlooked, however, is the significance of the role that HR must play in creating such cross-unit synergies. These often are most dramatically played out when it comes to questions of talent movement. For example, at Deutsche Telekom (see Chapter One), HR realized that the company's wide range of businesses, coupled with their global scale, created the potential to provide exceptional career opportunities, but to deliver on that potential, the company had to do a lot of work to create a corporate talent-management system. The resulting synergy did not come about automatically from the size of the organization. It came about through HR's active efforts to create an infrastructure that would enable cross-unit transfers of talent. For another and somewhat different example, see the case of Khazanah Nasional (Chapter Eight).

Mechanisms for Integration and Synergy

The cases in this book illustrate several mechanisms that help achieve integration and synergy. Here are five of the most powerful:

1. *Anchoring on broader goals.* Goals such as diversity, innovation, customer-centricity, and global brands can serve as touchstones to help various parts of an organization consider where and why they are working together, and where increased integration and synergy make the most sense.

2. *Using common logical frameworks.* HR organizations can use logical frameworks such as competencies, career paths, talent-supply chains, and process models as ways to identify where greater integration might produce valuable synergy. Frequently the organization has already identified areas where there are constraints on a process or talent flow, or where a common language about talent would help units improve their sharing of needed human capital. By capitalizing on these

insights, HR leaders can identify synergy opportunities and the value they might create.

3. *Using common data and technology.* In some organizations, common data about key human capital attributes can unearth synergy and integration opportunities. In the Deutsche Telekom case, for example (Chapter One), a common technological architecture provided a foundation for the analytical rigor and transparency needed for integration and synergy. At RBS (Chapter Eleven), a single global employee opinion survey provided a way of gaining insight into human capital.

4. *Having top leaders intervene directly.* In many cases, a catalyst for integration and synergy is the insistence by top leaders, or even boards of directors, that the organization direct itself to an overarching goal. This is particularly evident in the financial services industries. The shock of the economic down- turn, and the realization that decades-old systems may have induced destructive behaviors, led several organizations to com- mit themselves to integrative goals such as becoming a "helpful" bank and a contributor to the community. Savvy HR leaders will see such events as a chance to do more than simply support the initiative with HR programs and will also use it to build integration and synergy around broader themes.

5. *Sharing ideas and information.* Perhaps the most straight- forward route to synergy is simply the sharing of ideas. We will see in the RBS case in Chapter Eleven how the creation of Human Capital Online created a way for geographically dis- persed HR units to benefit from the HR know-how that existed across the organization. And in the case of Khazanah Nasional (Chapter Eight), forums were initiated for sharing ideas and experiences so that government-linked companies could benefit from belonging to a network of organizations. Neither RBS nor Khazanah Nasional invested in expensive knowledge-sharing mechanisms, but they did create places—one electronic, the other in face-to-face mode—where sharing could happen.

Knowing When Synergy Exists and When It Does Not

One important insight that comes with recognizing the value of integration is the realization that sometimes it is not worth the cost. The principle of optimization applies as well to synergy and integration as it does to everything else. HR leaders do little to help their organizations by creating integration where it does no good or, even worse, where it does harm.

Yes, well-targeted sharing of talent across business units can create value through career development and cross-unit competency building, but forcing units to share talent when those advantages do not exist may create costs and institutional friction that can actually detract from value. For example, research by Toshihiro Kanai, a professor of organizational behavior at Kobe University in Japan, found that a leading U.S. investment bank made a deliberate decision not to use cross-unit transfers because this kind of movement is not conducive to the intense specialization found in investment banking. The synergy opportunity that might have existed in a different kind of organization did not exist in the same way in investment banking.

Similarly, well-targeted integration across HR functional areas has the potential to create programs that reinforce each other, but forced integration for its own sake can create useless restrictions that prevent individual HR functions from achieving their best outcomes. Integration should be valued, but not without a keen awareness of the costs.

Silos sometimes exist for a reason. It can be highly efficient and effective for units to work independently. That is why we frame this principle not simply in terms of integration but in terms of how integration leads to *synergy*. When integration does not lead to synergy, it may well lead to $1 + 1 = 0$, where the costs of integration are not offset by its benefits.

Shanda is a gaming company with a unique approach to talent management that achieves integration across HR functions and across business units. As you read the following case, notice how the idea of applying the powerful community-building power of an online game fostered a natural environment for exploring and discovering where HR programs could work together. As a result, important organizational outcomes were created, and individual organizational units found themselves able to collaborate in creating a degree of success that was greater than what they could have achieved alone. Notice as well how shared data, the involvement of top leaders, interwoven HR programs, and the use of frameworks from other functional areas all combined to create a unique example of synergy through integration.

Shanda Interactive Entertainment, Ltd.: The Talent-Management Game

In China, with society undergoing extraordinary change in the past few decades, organizations now seek new ways to compete for talent and get the best from their people. The world of young Chinese contrasts sharply with the one their parents grew up in and is vastly different even from the China of ten years ago. At a time like this, suitable management models to copy may not exist, and so there is fertile soil for creating something new.

Shanda Interactive Entertainment is one of China's largest operators of online games. It also operates an online movie, literature, and music business. With nearly half a billion registered accounts, at any time an average of more than a million people are online playing *AION*, *Dungeons & Dragons*, *The Sign*, or other Shanda games. Given the nature of its businesses, it is not surprising that its employee population is young— the average age is just twenty-four. What is the best way to inspire, direct, and reward employees so young? How can they be retained when the growing economy presents unlimited temptations to join another firm? Shanda invented an unusual solution.

Understanding the Talent Segment

Normally when an organization thinks about talent segmentation, it makes distinctions within its own workforce, such as distinguishing the needs of workers in one region from those in another. In Shanda's case, it was more about understanding how its workforce differed from those around them. We think of this as supply-side segmentation.

Think for a moment about other talent segments that might exist in China and serve as the model for talent-management policies. There is an older generation immersed in the more traditional bureaucracy of the state-owned enterprises. There are the masses of poorly educated workers deployed in huge factories. There are people who grew up in hardship and struggled for a better life. None of these groups has much in common with the hip, tech-savvy, well-off generation of young employees driving Shanda's success.

What is this talent segment like? Shanda recognizes that they want transparency, independence, and opportunity. They want excitement. For them, life is a little like the online games they grew up on—full of adventure, opportunity, and instant rewards. In fact, online games are just as extraordinary a phenomenon in China as they are elsewhere in the world. Young people put enormous effort into mastering the games, toiling long hours to solve problems and overcome challenges. They often work as teams and pay hard-earned money to play. Maybe it was not surprising that a game company realized that if its young workers were extraordinarily motivated by games, then a talent-management system totally integrated around game-based concepts was the way to go.

Game On

Founded in 1999, Shanda grew rapidly. But while its games were innovative, its HR systems remained traditional. The systems were not especially effective, and they did not seem well suited to a generation of young employees who wanted more control over their own development.

In 2007, Chen Tianqiao, the company's chairman, CEO, and president, wondered why an employer could not engage employees' passion for their work the same way their passion was engaged by online games. He was struck by the fact that Shanda paid people well and they still left the company, whereas when it came to Shanda games, players were paying Shanda, and it was hard to drag them away from the games. If games are built on a point system, and players are motivated by the challenge of the gaming environment, maybe that same experience could provide the foundation for an integrated talent-management scheme.

Chen based his game approach on three keywords he felt reflected the value and nature of the experience of working at Shanda: *humanity, joy,* and *harmony.* While these terms may seem odd choices to an American or European, they tie to deep cultural roots that still resonate with his young workers.

Humanity refers to the individual's experience of working at Shanda, where people should treat each other well, in a spirit of common humanity. *Joy* comes from the pleasure of an employee's applying his or her skills to valuable Shanda projects. And *harmony* would come from the collective joy of all individuals working in concert with each other as virtual teams throughout the company. Talent management would be built around accumulating points, but these cultural anchors reminded people that something more important was at stake than just doing well at the game.

How a Game Delivers Integration and Synergy

Chen's concept of bringing ideas from the world of online games to the world of talent management was thrilling, but how on earth could it be done? The key step was to think in a more granular manner about work than we are used to. Traditionally, we think in terms of jobs and annual appraisals of how those jobs are done, with talent-management and reward systems aligned to those appraisals. But games do not work on some long-term assessment of how the player is doing; players get points based on achieving certain tasks. The heart of the Shanda talent-management system is to award points for the ongoing, day-to-day achievement of tasks, with management ensuring that individual tasks align with their strategic priorities and the work required to run the company on a day-to-day basis.

Shanda employees are awarded *ordinary* experience points (EXP) based on daily performance of their main jobs, and *extra* EXP based on additional accomplishments. They earn these extra points by joining an existing project, initiating a new project, taking on some additional tasks, or contributing to various kinds of knowledge sharing to enhance the collective capability of the organization.

The number of points that can be earned from these extra projects is set by a committee that ensures all projects align with the company's business plans and priorities. Higher-value projects earn more points. Here we have a function—alignment of an individual's work with company goals—normally performed by the performance-management system, but at Shanda it is simply built into the game. Contributing to important goals allows employees to earn more EXP than they would get from working on less important goals.

Employees can also lose points if they do their work badly or make mistakes. And if they lose enough points, it will affect their pay. This may seem harsh, but this penalty is soon over with—employees do not wait all year for a performance review, worrying that one misstep will color their whole appraisal—and they have an opportunity to take on a new project and earn those points back.

If employees get enough points, they get to move up a level, just as they would in a game. There are one hundred levels, and so there can be a lot of "promotion in place," with people moving up a salary level without necessarily moving into a different job. More significant career moves, such as moving from a senior technician to a professor, or a manager to a vice president, must be approved by an assessment committee.

Moving up a game level drives a pay increase currently set at around 20 percent. The game is designed so that a good junior employee should be able to go up a level in one year simply based on his or her ordinary EXPs. Just as in a game, the effort to go from one level to the next gets harder as the employee moves higher up the ladder. Here we have a system of annual increments, as well as the notion of progressing up a job ladder, falling out as a natural result of the EXP system.

Unlike the virtual world where almost anything is possible, there are some constraints on the talent-management game at Shanda. Points to be earned and distributed are not unlimited. Every department has a points budget, and the allocation of points is based on a committee review—a process seen by employees as far better than one where rewards and development are based on the subjective opinion of just one manager.

What is remarkable about this system from a talent-management perspective is that the gaming environment and the mathematical elegance of the point system mean that employees' pay, development, knowledge sharing, and citizenship behaviors are all translated into the common currency of game points. The trick to effective integration is to set up the point system and its surrounding governance structure to keep everything in balance, motivating appropriate attention to basic performance while also encouraging growth and citizenship. That way, the pay system, development system, and performance-management system more naturally work together to create something more than the sum of their parts. Contrast this to how often organizations have poorly connected systems where the reward system might actually discourage knowledge sharing, or work on projects outside the employee's standard role is ignored when it comes time to appraise performance.

For employees, the transparency that this system provides allows them to plot how to advance their career. Each employee's home page on the company intranet allows them to tell at a glance what projects they have completed, what projects are still pending, and what they have to achieve to qualify for the next level of their careers, bonuses, or salary increase. The process also naturally brings high-performing employees to the attention of management. One employee moved up sixteen levels in one year through the points he earned. Shanda does not need a separate talent-management process to spot this person as a high potential.

Keeping It Fresh

This program, which is administered by only four people within Shanda's HR department, is like any other game in that it needs tweaking every now and then to keep it interesting. Again, Shanda's HR staff learns from those who do it better than almost anyone else in the world—their own game designers. The Shanda game designers refresh their games once a quarter to keep attracting customers, and so HR finds new ways to keep their own game fresh as well. New challenges are announced quarterly, such as assignments to write articles or reports that would then be judged by the Shanda community.

Shanda is now rolling out a game version based on the idea of a virtual city; every employee has a city of his or her own. With each project or task completed, the employee is awarded some new virtual objects with which to decorate his or her city. Buildings, flower beds, trees, stars—anything that could be seen in a city landscape could be an award for a job well done. The more accomplished the employee, the more lavishly outfitted the city is. Each city owner is even able to express his or her own mood of the day by deciding what the city's weather is. By scanning all the cities from its own vantage point, HR can see at a glance the overall mood of the Shanda employees at any given moment.

In talking about employees designing their own virtual cities, we seem to have strayed a long way from the familiar practices of talent management. Yet it flows very naturally given the logic of online gaming and trying, element by element, to create that same dynamic in the workplace. Shanda is not afraid of going where this logic leads them, even if it is highly unconventional. While the idea of virtual cities might feel bizarre to a middle-class manager in Manchester, it is absolutely a natural means of personal expression for a tech-savvy twenty-something in Shanghai. Shanda knows its talent segment, and company leaders use that knowledge to tailor an integrated talent-management system that works for them.

The One Thing You Should Take Away

It is natural to want to maximize the things that are closest to us, whether it is ourselves, our team, our function, our division, or our region. But having perspective means taking the wider view. Asking how things fit together and where they could work better in combination is often the key to a whole that is much more than the sum of its parts. Maximizing anything without concern for how it affects other things is a recipe for waste and conflict.

5

"SPREADING PEANUT BUTTER" OR OPTIMIZING INVESTMENTS?

> *Optimization* follows from segmentation and is about exploiting the differences between employee groups to enable the organization to realize the optimal value exchange between itself and a particular group. It means identifying where and how certain investments will yield an excess return while minimizing or eliminating investments that are underperforming.

Optimization sounds like an engineering word for common sense. If the optimal route to the village is to walk through the glade, why would anyone take the suboptimal route through the swamp? Yet suboptimal decisions are made all the time. This may be because of a lack of awareness of the options ("We didn't know there was a glade"), tradition ("We have always walked through the swamp to get to the village"), or factors related to emotion ("We have invested a lot in our swamp boots and will feel bad if we don't use them").

Optimization means investing resources in ways that achieve the greatest impact on success for the amount invested. This goes beyond simply achieving a positive financial return or demonstrating that an investment pays off. Optimization also means having the insight and the courage to know when to reduce the investment in something that has worked in the past but no longer produces the greatest return. According to Boudreau and Ramstad in *Beyond HR* (2007, pp. 39–40):

> Many HR decisions try to increase learning, engagement or retention without limit or context. This is very different from

optimizing a portfolio of HR practices against the organization's unique resource opportunity costs and constraints. For example, if more sales training increases product knowledge, which increases selling success, a less mature decision framework might apply training more broadly. Having proved the value of training by linking it to increased sales, the right decision seems to be to do more training.

In fact, considering the necessary investments (time, money, etc.) to achieve increased selling success through training, enhancing product knowledge from an already high level may be very expensive. The optimal solution might involve less product knowledge and more motivation, and thus less training and more incentives.

Optimization certainly means setting priorities, unearthing the highest-impact HR investments, and shifting resources to them. It is more subtle than that, however. It also involves making the right level of investments across an array of potential opportunities, with each getting its proper amount and the entire portfolio working together. Think about how a personal financial portfolio is constructed, where sufficient investments are in different asset classes, with the goal of an optimal risk-return relationship. Yes, priorities may change from stocks to bonds to cash as investment objectives or conditions change. Nevertheless, such shifts do not mean simply moving the portfolio to whatever asset class seems most promising. Rather, these shifts involve knowing when to maintain investments in the fundamentals (such as basic life insurance) while putting resources toward promising new areas as conditions merit.

The same holds for human capital decisions and investments. Optimization does not mean simply showing that HR adds value or provides valuable services. It more often involves having the courage and insight to know just how much to invest in the "nuts and bolts" so that the basics, such as payroll and benefits transactions, are handled with sufficient quality, but not too high or too low a degree of quality. Getting that balance right provides the license to explore more advanced high-payoff opportunities.

Optimization is deeply related to the principle of segmentation. Indeed, it makes little sense to analyze the differences in the supply and demand relationships for different talent segments if you are not willing to invest in ways that reflect those differences and to use them to create strategic value. It is also not possible to fully optimize when you are not willing to invest differently in different segments. The "peanut butter" approach—equal spreading of the same human capital programs across every group of employees—is seldom optimal.

Optimization is also deeply related to integration and synergy. True optimization does not mean investing in individual HR programs with high payoffs but instead means combining HR programs so that each complements the others. It means investing less in some HR programs when pushing too hard would undermine their synergy with others. It also involves optimizing the array of HR programs across organizational units to create synergy in how talent moves across them, even if each unit does not necessarily have HR programs maximally customized to its particular requirements.

The next generation of HR practice will be much more hard-nosed in pressing the question "Is this the optimal choice?" HR professionals will ask this question first rather than simply making choices that generate few objections, or that can be individually justified because their value exceeds their cost. As Boudreau and Ramstad (2007) point out, this is precisely the evolution that caused the finance discipline to emerge from the professional practice of accounting, and the marketing discipline to emerge from the professional practice of advertising. Similarly, Boudreau (2010) has shown that well-accepted management frameworks, such as portfolio theory, supply-chain management, lean manufacturing, and product design, have optimization at the heart of their analytical logic. If HR is to evolve to a position of similar stature and influence, it must also make optimization a central pillar.

The Optimization Mind-Set

HR always wants to make the best choices, but traditionally HR leaders have not been tasked with optimizing choices in the way an engineering department or an investment manager would be. This opens up a great opportunity for HR to raise its game.

Although there are specific tools to bring to the task of optimization, the greater element is mind-set. HR leaders can make asking about optimization a natural way of approaching their work, even though no one has asked them to. As we have seen from other functions' experiences with optimization, once business leaders see that HR can be optimized, they will start asking for that.

To take a familiar example, organizational leaders now routinely accept the idea that optimal investments in leadership development require both segmentation and integration. High-potential leaders receive different opportunities and challenges than others, and the combination of rewards, development, and staffing is designed to work together. If high-potential leaders are seen to need development as team players, then care is taken to ensure that rewards are not overly focused on individual performance and that development strikes the right balance of individual advancement and team-based experiences. Few investors or members of executive teams would accept an HR strategy that did not differentiate high-potential leaders from others or that failed to consider how all the elements of the program for high-potential leaders fit together.

Yet, as Boudreau and Ramstad (2007) have noted, the realm of high-potential leaders is often unique in its attention to optimization. The same principles can also apply to many other areas of the organization, with quite good effects. Forward-thinking organizations optimize by investing differently in frontline leaders and customer-facing associates. They organize those investments around such themes as diversity, customer-centricity, and leading global brands. They require that different HR functions consider how their programs work together rather than simply how each function will achieve best practice or sufficient return on investment.

But this kind of clear choice is not actually typical of HR work. The more typical approach is that senior executives discover or become convinced that such issues as diversity or a global employment brand are important and then ask HR to address them with improvements. The HR function then implements broad-based programs of engagement, training, rewards, and development aimed at increasing diversity or awareness of the global employment brand. HR does this without pushing back or asking, "Where does global brand really matter most? Where is an investment in diversity or inclusion going to make the most difference?" Optimization means having the knowledge that certain employee segments (for example, frontline leaders in retail banking) may benefit more than others from such investments. It also means having the courage to allocate disproportionate resources to those segments. Does this mean that diversity or global brand is not universally valuable? No, we are not denying they have value, but that's not the right question. The optimization question is "Where would improving these things make the biggest difference to our sustainable strategic success?"

Perhaps the most notorious example of this problem was the rush among organizations to implement forced-distribution systems for performance assessment because Jack Welch, the CEO at General Electric (GE), was using that kind of system in the 1980s and 1990s, when GE was achieving enviable growth and returns. This type of system identifies the top 20 percent, the middle 70 percent, and the bottom 10 percent of performers. A moment of reflection will reveal, however, that draconian efforts to identify and weed out the bottom 10 percent are appropriate only in certain circumstances, and that an optimal approach will tailor this kind of performance management to those circumstances. As Conaty and Charan (2010) point out, GE's success often owed far more to an intimate, tailored approach than to a rigid, across-the-board application of policy.

Instead of simply providing what is asked for, HR can reframe issues with an optimization mind-set, saying, in effect, "We have expertise in finding optimal solutions to people-related issues. Let us do that rather than jump to implementing programs." HR needs to take a teaching role with respect to the CEO as opposed to being an order taker. HR ought to be examining and illustrating the choices so that the organization makes optimal use of scarce resources.

As we said earlier, organizational leaders often approach people-related issues with nonoptimal frameworks, saying, "We need the best possible performer in every role" or "We need to reduce turnover as much as possible" or "Everyone in this organization must be customer-focused." In fact, however, improvements in such things as performance, turnover, and customer-centricity often have much greater effects in some areas than in others, and the right investment approach may be to make such improvements where they will matter most and avoid trying to make these improvements where things are already good enough, or where improvements would make less difference.

Retooling HR means educating leaders to see that nice-sounding traditional guidelines can be used more effectively if an approach is taken that is more closely aligned with such optimization-focused business models as engineering tolerances, bottleneck analysis, and market segmentation. Good CEOs will want HR to stand up and tell them when the solutions they are suggesting are wrong. HR needs to build in awareness of the optimization mind-set to discover what the choices are. HR can help organizational leaders become aware that there is a path through the glade, and HR can then lead the organization onto the best path rather than cheerfully helping leaders march across the swamp simply because a trek through the swamp will get them to the village and the swamp is the route they have always taken.

Smart and Tough Choices

If the first step toward optimization is taking the time to dig deeply into the options, an equally important second step is making the options palatable and actionable. This is the heart of evidence-based change, which emphasizes that it is not enough just to know the answer, it is about motivating strategic change. Even something as well accepted as focused and differential investment in high-potential employees still generates some discomfort. Many organizations hesitate to tell high-potential employees that they have high potential, largely because it means telling other employees that they do not. We see exactly the same phenomenon when managers are asked to optimize the use of their reward dollars by differentiating on the basis of performance. Managers frequently prefer the comfortable choice of spreading reward dollars around rather than the optimal choice of putting those dollars where they will make the greatest difference to the long-term success of the organization.

An organization may decide to pay marketing analysts much more than financial analysts who do an equivalent job simply because, at a particular time, improving marketing analysts' performance or the availability of talent for marketing roles is more pivotal. This sort of choice can be hard for HR professionals who were raised on the notion of equal treatment as a fundamental pillar of their profession. Fairness, however, carefully considered, is not the same as equal treatment across the board.

Cases may also arise in which the company needs to reward moderate performers simply because they have skills that are hard to replace. In developing economies, for example, it may take a long time to find engineers who have high technical skills as well as experience in global marketing. Given this hiring challenge, it may make sense to give high rewards to engineers who have technical skills only, simply in order to retain those engineers, even though they clearly fall short of the ideal skill set. By contrast, for job areas where there is an available population of fully skilled applicants, high pay for those with incomplete skill sets is unlikely to be optimal. In essence, the organization applies a different standard to the scarce engineers than to people in other jobs. It takes a serious optimization mind-set to see things this way.

Optimization may also be about making other kinds of tough trade-offs. If strategic plans for growth in South America mean that the organization needs to dramatically increase the number of leaders on the management team who have experience in these countries, then the optimal decision may be to focus diversity efforts on increasing the representation of Spanish and Portuguese leaders. This would be instead of simply creating a new diversity program applied across the board and might mean shifting resources out of gender diversity, for example, to this new initiative. Making such trade-offs is hard, but it is essential to make them carefully, and with very firm, logical rationales.

Optimization often requires such tough choices. Smart choices and tough choices depend on the right approach, whether analytical or social in nature.

Analytical Approaches to Optimization

As we have seen, perhaps the most important tool for optimization is reframing the way leaders inside and outside HR think about the objectives of their human resource investments. Simply restating a decision to emphasize optimization rather than description or evaluation can have significant effects. For example, instead of asking only "What is important?" ask "Where would improving something make the biggest difference to success?" This kind of reframing can dramatically refocus decisions on the optimal solution.

To support this change in mind-set, there are emerging tools that specifically reflect optimization. These tools are often based on accepted tools from other management disciplines where optimization is more accepted and has a longer history. Thus "retooling HR" (Boudreau, 2010) can be a potent approach toward optimization.

The sections that follow offer examples of analytical approaches to optimization. These examples are not meant to be comprehensive, but they do offer a starting point for readers to consider where they might find further examples of analytical approaches to optimization. The example of the Royal Bank of Scotland Group, at the end of this chapter, also provides specific illustrations of several ways in which measurement and data can be optimized.

Finding Variability in Unexpected Places Variability is a good friend of optimization. Wherever there is a wide performance distribution, there is the opportunity to get more of the high end and less of the low end. The Royal Bank of Scotland Group, for example, found optimization opportunities by noticing that there was wide performance variation in its retail locations (that is, its branches), even after such traditional factors as location, customer base, and product offerings were taken into account. That simple observation suggested that it might be possible to better optimize branch returns by looking for factors that explained the variation. For this organization, measurable human capital factors explained a significant amount of the difference among branches. That discovery suggested ways to optimize measurement as well as HR investments. The result was to reduce the amount of low performance and thus increase the proportion of high performance. As a general principle, if performance varies in unexpected ways, that is a clue to optimization opportunities.

Optimizing Offerings to Fit Real Preferences Marketers are always immersed in the problem of deciding which product features matter most to customers. For example, do customers care so much about having a lightweight notebook computer that they are willing to accept a trade-off on its durability? Would they rather have long battery life than speedy performance? Would they prefer a cheaper plastic case to a more fashionable aluminum one? In the same way, HR and organizational leaders must make sense of an increasingly customizable set of potential employment offerings, arrayed against an ever more demanding and diverse employee base. Should we offer pet-grooming services to our employees who are pet owners? How about virtual work opportunities to our millennials?

Marketers have long relied on a technique called *conjoint analysis* to analyze the trade-offs customers make when they are faced with choices among packages of different features. The same technique, in combination with portfolio theory, has been applied to understanding how employee populations make trade-offs among employment features when they consider whether to stay, perform, and engage. Boudreau (2010) describes this technique in detail, and it has long been utilized by Towers Watson to help organizations optimize their investments in total rewards. Our purpose here is not to provide a detailed explanation of conjoint analysis, but Figure 5.1 shows how powerful this technique can be for optimization. The figure shows the analysis of four portfolios in connection with Microsoft's "efficient frontier" of combinations of the reward elements that optimize costs against retention. Each reward combination on the curve represents the maximum retention that can be achieved for a given investment in total rewards, with each point representing a particular combination of reward elements. Notice how this approach differs both from the approach of simply maximizing employee retention by providing the highest level of rewards (this approach is not optimal because it over-rewards when less would do) and from the approach of simply matching market-level rewards (this approach, too, is not optimal because it does not take employees' preferences into account).

Figure 5.1 Optimizing Rewards

Mircosoft's "efficient frontier" of optimum rewards and retention

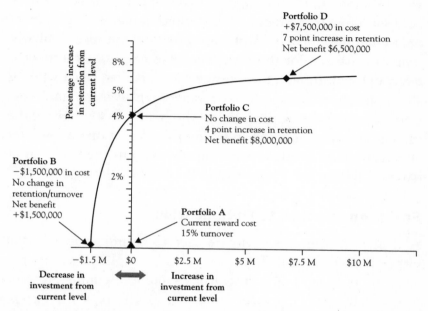

Source: Adapted from Allen L. Slade, Thomas O. Davenport, Darryl R. Roberts, and Shamir Shah, "How Microsoft Optimized Its Investment in People After the Dot-Com Era," *Journal of Organizational Excellence*, 22(1), 2002, p. 51.

Optimizing Turnover and Supply Chains What are optimal levels of employee shortages or surpluses? The answer from HR's clients is often "Zero shortages or surpluses, just the right number of employees." What is the optimal level of employee turnover? The answer from HR's clients is often "As low as possible to avoid turnover costs." But when the same questions are applied to such resources as raw materials or unfinished goods, the answers are much different. Operations management, marketing, and manufacturing have long recognized that optimizing a resource may mean tolerating shortages or surpluses in parts of the supply chain if the costs of doing so would be less than the costs of trying to avoid shortages and surpluses.

For example, if there is an ample supply of replacement materials available at low cost, then it may be a good idea to allow shortages that can be filled quickly. If replacement materials are in short or uncertain supply, however, it may make sense to hold surpluses as insurance against running out. Trying to manage for zero shortages or surpluses is often not optimal. Similarly, trying to manage for the lowest possible employee turnover is rarely optimal. In fact, turnover can even be beneficial when it allows the organization to make room for replacement employees who are more valuable than those who have left. Optimizing the staffing process requires abandoning the idea of one answer for all situations and instead tailoring strategies to the situation at hand (Boudreau, 2010; Cascio and Boudreau, 2010).

Social Approaches to Optimization

At least half the battle with respect to optimization is social rather than technical. It means getting people to accept the logic of change, not just calculate more accurate answers. Fortunately, social approaches are where HR typically excels. Here are some social approaches that make optimization more successful:

- *Build trust*. If HR's instinct has been that trust is a critical cultural trait, then a look at the challenges of optimization confirms this. If people trust that decisions really are being driven by sound logic and not by sloppy thinking or politics, then it will be easier to get their buy-in on tough choices.

- *Enhance transparency*. The data and logic behind an optimization decision should be open to scrutiny and challenge. The reason for a decision needs to be transparent to all.

- *Communicate*. Explicitly making optimization an HR tool is a new idea for many organizations. HR needs to communicate—up, down, and across the organization—what it is doing. (For a great example of transparency in communication, see the case of CME Group, in Chapter Two.)

- *Delegitimize the status quo.* One of the main arguments against making choices is simply that people are content with the status quo. "Don't make waves" remains a popular piece of advice. To raise its game, HR needs top organizational leaders to visibly support the view that maintaining the status quo is not a legitimate strategy. HR needs top leaders to insist on rigorous choices and enable a culture of change. Every more optimal strategy was at its inception a break from standard procedure. By definition, it is hard to optimize if you just copy what everyone else is doing.

- *Redefine fairness.* Fairness and equality are not the same. If the organization needs certain skills more than others, then those skills are what the organization should pay for. If one talent pool is more critical to the future than another, then the more critical pool will get more investment. If a beloved program is no longer the best use of scarce resources, then it is not fair to keep that program going and starve more essential programs.

We should be careful not to paint a grim view of optimization. Usually optimization decisions will be warmly greeted, and stakeholders will be impressed that HR has approached issues with new thoughtfulness and rigor. Nevertheless, there is a need to be alert to the risks of disaffection with optimization choices, and to deploy social approaches that will *optimize*, not minimize, the risks involved.

Royal Bank of Scotland Group: Optimizing Measurement

HR metrics are notoriously difficult to get right. HR books and articles are full of recommended metrics, and these can easily number in the hundreds. Deciding which metrics to track is essentially an optimization question. Each of the hundreds of possible metrics has some potential value, and the challenge for HR is to find a way to focus attention on some subset of that number. The Royal Bank of Scotland (RBS) Group, a global financial services organization based in the United Kingdom, demonstrated its commitment to HR measurement when it established a dedicated employee research and insights function, Human Capital Strategy. The challenge for the Human Capital Strategy group, under the leadership of Greig Aitken, was to figure out what to deliver under its broad mandate to provide HR metrics.

Starting with What Matters

A big decision Aitken needed to make at the outset was whether to cast a wide net and capture many metrics or simply pick a few key measures. If RBS wanted to be able to efficiently produce a wide range of HR metrics, it would first have to build an exceptional data infrastructure. It can be tempting for a large organization to go for a global technology infrastructure that would let it produce whatever kind of HR metrics the businesses might want. However, for Aitken, the risk involved in a project of that magnitude was just too great. He had seen other organizations go down the route of trying to build the ultimate HR data warehouse, and years later they were still up to their neck in technology issues rather than using HR metrics to support the business.

Having made the decision to forgo a technology-driven approach, that still left the challenge of deciding how many and which of the hundreds of possible metrics to gather. Aitken's decision was based in part on what he had seen at board presentations by marketing and finance.

"Whenever marketing and finance came in to make their presentations," Aitken says, "they would have hundreds of pages of data but would only talk about two or three key measures. We decided to jump straight to identifying the key measures for HR."

The attitude of aiming for just the few *best* measures, rather than a broader range of *good* measures, is characteristic of optimization decisions. If we think of the Human Capital Strategy group as an ice cream stall, they were planning to offer the three most popular flavors, not everything customers might want.

What members of the Human Capital Strategy group were looking for were measures comparable to marketing's "customer service index" or finance's "sales over target"—numbers that would help the business deeply understand the effectiveness of the people strategy and demonstrably set apart the business performance.

The idea that the measures should be focused on the business hardly seems extraordinary, but a great deal of the conversation on HR metrics is not focused on improving the business so much as justifying what HR is doing. There is a great deal of interest in the HR profession in gathering metrics around the return on investment (ROI) of training to justify training budgets or cost-of-hire data to justify buying a new applicant-tracking system. Using the optimization lens, we might say RBS was looking to optimize on the business impact of HR metrics rather than optimize on which metrics would have the biggest direct impact on the HR budget.

The approach to discovering the most important flavors of HR metrics was through thorough research. RBS worked with Nitnin Noria and Boris Groysberg at the Harvard Business School to study the issue, and then spent time in Chicago with the Organization Surveys and Insights team of Towers Watson to do the serious statistics (Cronbach's alphas, Comparative Fit Index, Non-Normed Fit Index) needed to prove the measures they intended to use really were valid.

"We reached the important but not new conclusion that two lead indicators, in terms of superior sustainable business value in customer service, are great leaders and highly engaged staff. Underneath those two measures are the hundreds of activities that contribute to it."

What was important in this case was not that they had discovered something surprising but that they could prove it mattered. They knew it would be optimal to focus attention narrowly on these key measures and could defend their decision in front of the businesses that otherwise might not pay attention to the metrics or argue for different ones.

Optimizing Responsiveness

While the Human Capital Strategy group was able to focus attention on the most important metrics, that did not eliminate the need for benchmarking against other HR metrics.

"Of course, we like to be responsive to the businesses," says Aitken. "But if you tried to respond to all their requests for measures, whether it be total turnover, voluntary turnover, short-term tenure, high-potential turnover—hundreds of different metrics—you would suddenly find you had a team of ten to fifteen people trying to reactively respond to the businesses' insatiable appetite for external benchmarks."

One simple process to balance optimization with responsiveness to customers was to establish an annual exercise where HR would sit down with each business to discuss what metrics were most important and whom to benchmark against. By looking at requests in a systematic way instead of responding in an ad hoc manner, they were able to join up all the requests into one single report. It is a good example of HR proactively taking control of an area so that trade-offs can be consciously made instead of simply trying to provide service in response to ongoing requests from their internal customers.

Optimizing What the Board Sees

A final example of optimization with respect to HR metrics at RBS shows up in HR's work with the board. Historically, they had been taking data from the employee survey and presenting insights on about fifty key areas like efficiency, risk, and performance management in a big presentation. "We would provide them with all the interesting information," Aitken explains. "Then we'd basically say, 'Catch,' and they had to work out what to do about the findings."

No one was saying that parts of the data were irrelevant or uninteresting. But clearly this was not the best use of the board's time. Again the underlying question was "Are we better off just investing time in understanding a few things rather than spreading our attention over many things?"

"We did a lot of key-factor analysis to find what the real drivers were for three issues—restoration of pride, divisional leadership, and employee engagement," Aitken says. "Those were the three areas that were crucially important to the organization's strategic plan. We effectively reengineered the way we provide insight to our businesses so that we are able to give them, in order of impact, the top four, five, or six things that will enable change and improve leadership capability in their units."

The One Thing You Should Take Away

Smart HR departments think hard about what mix of investments will have the optimal payoff. This can be hard because it may mean cutting back on some well-liked programs in favor of investments where there is a higher return or investing more in one group of employees than another. But fairness and equality are not the same, because equal treatment in the face of different needs or returns will unfairly penalize some and over-reward others. The "fairest" idea is that differential HR investments are the only way to fairly reflect the contributions and returns of both employees and the organization. Have the courage to invest differently when it makes sense, and the capacity to explain the differences clearly.

Part Two

SIX IN-DEPTH CASES OF EVIDENCE-BASED CHANGE

6

ROYAL BANK OF CANADA'S HR PARTNERSHIP

If an organization takes HR seriously, you can be confident they will develop a strong HR department, have good programs, and maybe pick up a few awards along the way. The Royal Bank of Canada (RBC) has all that, yet there is something more that is hard to put a finger on. At RBC, HR themes mingle with business themes, to the point where it is hard to tell if you are listening to an HR tune or a business one. After partnering with HR on various initiatives over the years, the business has gone beyond supporting HR programs to having internalized the thinking behind them. This is the new frontier in business partnership for the HR profession.

It is helpful to understand a bit about RBC. RBC is not just a company. It has long been a pillar of the Canadian economy. It is among the largest banks in the world, as measured by market capitalization, and is the largest financial institution in Canada. RBC employs approximately 80,000 full- and part-time people in Canada, the United States, and 53 other countries. It has a long history and is well known for managerial excellence and stability.

The HR function prefers not to see the business as its "customer" to whom they deliver services. Rather, they frame the relationship as a partnership.

"A great partner provides service, but they do much more," said Zabeen Hirji, chief human resources officer. "Being responsive to the needs that are articulated is table stakes. We try to go further into the value chain and understand what the business wants to achieve and where the gaps are. Then we provide advice and develop talent solutions to get there. Partnering has a longer-term time horizon. It's about joint accountability for sustainable performance."

A recurring theme in how RBC operates is their emphasis on common goals and values. Regulatory changes around compensation could lead to a sense that HR sits on one side of the table, thinking about compliance, while the business is on the other side, thinking about revenue. But at RBC they stress that HR and the business share the common goal of using reward in a way that optimizes motivation, performance, and retention while controlling risk. HR and a business partner may have different opinions on what to do, but the longer time horizons, and attention to common objectives, keep the partnership on track. Additionally, many people in HR have had line roles, and many people in line roles have had HR experience. That common ground makes it easier to stay aligned and to understand each other.

A deep sense of their partnership with the business shows up in areas like diversity and employee opinion surveys. In these areas in particular, RBC is a leader in HR best practices.

A Diversity Program That Thrives on Integration

Imagine that a family emigrates from Mumbai to Montreal, and one of the first things they do is go to a bank to open a savings account. In what way is this story about HR?

At RBC it most definitely is. For RBC their success at winning the business of newcomers to Canada is a natural consequence of their internal diversity programs—although one could just as easily say that at RBC their internal diversity programs are a natural consequence of their aim to serve customers.

The focus on diversity fits within a much broader strategic vision of always earning the right to be clients' first choice and goal of being a high-performing, customer-centric organization. Among the customers RBC wishes to serve are newcomers to Canada; it wants to be the financial institution of choice for newcomers and the cultural markets they represent. The bank works on making it easier for newcomers to get over the hurdles of becoming established financially after they arrive. To inform people about RBC's attention to newcomers, even before they immigrate, the bank has introduced a Web site aimed at potential immigrants and created a "Welcome to Canada" banking package in 14 languages.

At this point diversity sounds like a marketing initiative, but HR is deeply involved in driving the success of the program. HR assessed the languages spoken by their staff and proactively recruited to fill any gaps, and helped create a telephone service that can serve clients in over 150 languages. When a family arrives from Mumbai, chances are the RBC employees can serve them in the Marathi language. RBC clients can also find the nearest of 1,200 branches in Canada where employees speak their preferred language using an online tool. The workforce strategy and the marketing strategy are neatly aligned.

One thoughtful and early "out of the box" move HR made to smooth the hiring of a diverse workforce was to refrain from asking prospective employees to name the institution where they received their education during the preliminary employment screenings. This helped avoid inadvertent bias. Instead, credentials and education were verified much later in the hiring process. This attention to detail sets RBC apart. Now RBC sees the question of educational background as no longer about inadvertent bias and more about knowing the best schools internationally in order to secure the best candidates.

From a business perspective, this is HR supporting the newcomer initiative, but from an HR perspective it can be seen as simply one facet of creating a diverse workforce and an inclusive culture. It is perhaps not surprising that the HR group at RBC has been a leader in diversity. Toronto, where RBC has its headquarters, is one of the most ethnically diverse cities in the world. Torontonians traveling to other large cities, such as Berlin or Barcelona or Beijing, are often struck by the cultural homogeneity of those cities compared to what they are used to at home. RBC believed that to be good at serving this diverse client population, they would need to be good at attracting a diverse employee population.

The evidence for the value of a diverse employee population is readily seen in retail banking. There is no question that having people from an ethnic community in a branch enhances their success at doing business with that community. In Aboriginal banking, having Aboriginal staff is hugely important; it is the difference between being there and not being in the game at all. So diversity has never been just a feel-good initiative. It is, as RBC likes to say, the smart thing to do and the right thing to do.

But it is not just marketing, the retail business, and HR that work hand in hand on diversity. Like many other large organizations, RBC does charitable work to support the communities it serves. The group responsible for this work no doubt is inundated with ideas for good projects to fund, but because the idea of diversity is so ingrained in the business as a whole, the community work includes a newcomers' scholarship program for youth. The scholarship program encourages young people to further their education, which makes them better qualified for the kinds of jobs that RBC's HR leaders anticipate in the future. At the same time, the program enhances the RBC brand in the community, leading not only to more customers but also to a greater probability that qualified and diverse applicants will be attracted to RBC as their employer of choice. "Our best diversity work is when we make initiatives around employees, communities, and clients all work together," said Per Scott, vice president of human resources.

Attesting to the degree to which the different functions work together is a project called Diversity 2.0. There are many diversity initiatives in specific areas (for example, work in the Indian community and in the Chinese community), but the bank felt there was value in exploring a conceptual framework to tie these many individual efforts together in ways that would strengthen the RBC brand and unlock business opportunities. RBC recognized the increasing diversity of consumers, labor markets, and its workforce and sensed an evolution in perceptions about diversity—a shift from *having* diversity to *doing something with* diversity. To understand how consumers viewed diversity and inclusion, and how it can drive business value, marketing tested concepts and explored views of targeted client segments through online bulletin boards, focus groups, and surveys.

HR is funding the Diversity 2.0 project to develop the needed umbrella concepts, but this work is not done by HR. It is being done by marketing. They are the ones with expertise in focus groups and concept testing needed to create the right framework. HR guides the work, pays for it, and ultimately will leverage it throughout the company. Is Diversity 2.0 best seen as an HR project, or is it really more of a marketing project? Scott said, "We could list both marketing and HR reasons to do this work, and it makes sense from all sides. We don't need to decide which side is preeminent."

For RBC, diversity blends across all areas of the business, and it feels very natural to see it holistically instead of as an HR initiative. When Zabeen Hirji gives speeches, she is as likely to talk about diversity from the viewpoint of building business as from the viewpoint of hiring and developing a diverse workforce. "After this kind of speech," Hirji said, "people may ask why I, as an HR leader, am talking about the client side rather than the workforce side of diversity. It goes back to our belief in business partnering. There is a lot of white space out there between functions, and we don't have to be constrained by a traditional mandate. Good business leaders do what makes sense for the business. That's what guides us."

HR, as a partner, is comfortable in the white space trying to connect the dots between workforce, client, and community diversity strategies. It helps them take diversity to a different place.

Striving for Synergy

Large organizations are in favor of integrated efforts. But all too often it is hard to avoid fragmented efforts that seem fine individually but fail to reinforce—perhaps might even undermine—one another. Hirji says at RBC the fundamental sources of alignment that make integrated efforts like the diversity work possible are leadership, culture, and values.

At the top level, chief executive Gordon Nixon chairs the diversity leadership council, and it has always been business heads who set the tone of importance and accountability around the diversity work. It is that sort of leadership involvement that fostered the integrated approach to diversity.

However, it is not the sort of culture where the top leadership gives orders and the rest just do what they are told. The leadership sets the tone, but then it is up to people to figure out for themselves what needs to get done. In figuring that out, it is natural for HR to work directly with marketing, economics, and other groups. RBC's culture is collaborative, and there is no need for everything to be run up the hierarchy and back down again before different departments can work together. This ease of lateral communication aids synergy. We already saw how HR funds a joint marketing-HR diversity initiative. That sort of thing would be unheard of in many organizations but happens quite readily in the collaborative culture of RBC.

Finally, there are cohesive values and a shared vision that keep people aligned even when they do not sit down and discuss a particular issue together. For diversity, HR led the creation of an eleven-page "blueprint" that laid out how and why diversity matters and the roles different parts of the business can play. For example, priorities and objectives are laid out for "Talent and the Workforce," "Marketplace," and "Community," as are the elements that need to be in place to sustain diversity, such as stakeholder engagement, oversight, and transparency. Different parts of the blueprint will be relevant to different managers, but someone in recruiting will be referring to the same document as someone in economics and someone in marketing. The document is a simple integrating mechanism that helps various groups stay on track and see their role in the bigger picture.

Contrast RBC's highly integrated view of diversity to how diversity programs work in many other firms. There, all too often, recruitment will bump up diversity hiring only to find it is a revolving door because conditions are not in place to retain women and minorities. HR will strive to hit diversity targets that the operating business feels are good-hearted but get in the way of results. Their community programs go ahead, driven by some reasonable agenda, but one that does not create synergy with what HR or the business is doing. RBC, on the other hand, avoids these failures of alignment through integrating mechanisms of leadership, culture, and values.

Organizations seeking to emulate RBC's success in diversity should not focus on the list of programs HR has initiated but instead should incorporate the perspective that everything is deeply intertwined, and not a collection of independent pieces. At RBC we see leaders speaking on diversity, community affairs funding diversity programs, recruiting targeted to improve diversity, marketing programs aimed at certain ethnic groups, and so on. Everyone pays attention to diversity so that the overall approach creates synergy. There would be little point in RBC's sponsoring a job fair aimed at the lesbian, gay, bisexual, and transgender community without also considering visible community support by engaged company leaders, appropriate sponsorship opportunities, and investment in creating an inclusive environment. RBC pays attention to the whole picture.

From Diversity to Employee Opinion Surveys

We saw how the theme of diversity served to integrate programs within HR and the business. The same dynamic exists with employee opinion surveys (EOS). Business leaders will look at the EOS data and say, "It will be hard to achieve our strategic goals unless we get the employee engagement numbers up" or "We expect improved revenue to result from our investment in engagement programs." Just as with diversity, EOS is an initiative that is understood and valued by both the business and HR.

Business leaders and HR share a common logical understanding about how employee attitudes (including but not limited to measures of engagement) connect to business outcomes. They both recognize value in the trove of data EOS provides for decision making about their workforce and the business.

Most organizations will at least pay lip service to the idea of engagement, and managers will look at the data, but after a review, many managers will put the data in a drawer and get back to their "real" work. But at RBC, the managers believe the EOS is part of their real work; and the EOS data are business data, not just an HR report. One reason managers have come to this view is that HR focuses on meaning, not just data. Typically what comes out of these opinion surveys is a set of descriptive statistics about which factors are high, which are low, what has changed, and how the data compare to other organizations. This is a good start, but RBC has been doing opinion surveys for more than ten years and has taken the practice considerably further.

For example, RBC has invested a lot of time studying the relationship between EOS findings and branch performance. It's common for companies to cite how engagement drives performance, but RBC has dug deeper and found how important team effectiveness measures are in creating customer satisfaction in areas such as staff courtesy and a positive attitude. Another finding was that if employees felt trained and empowered, that showed up in customers' views about their competence, such as the ability of staff to answer questions and solve problems the first time around. The ongoing analysis has revealed many other insights that help improve branch performance.

It is a great idea to measure engagement. It is an important step to look for a relationship between engagement and business outcomes. But it's obvious that RBC has pushed logic-driven analytics far beyond those first steps. They are not content to come up with a simple relationship between overall engagement scores and branch performance that allows them to say, "Look!

HR programs matter to the business." They want to dig deeper into the data to find insights that are really useful to managers and the design of HR programs. They employ a deeper framework that asks, "What specific elements of HR investments and outcomes drive what specific elements of branch performance?" From this comes the insight that employee perceptions of competence and empowerment are not just generally related to branch performance, they are related specifically to customer reports of questions answered correctly and problems solved.

One interesting analysis involves looking at the employee value proposition from the viewpoint of source of hire. As it turns out, RBC discovered that employees hired right out of school care a lot about the caliber of people they work with, employees who came to RBC via an acquisition were concerned with opportunities to advance their career, while employees who were recruited from a competitor tended to focus on cash compensation.

Many organizations would not be able to do this cut of the data if they had not decided to ask about source of hire in the EOS. At RBC the survey is linked to the HR information system (in a way that preserves anonymity, of course) so that all the information about similar groups of employees is available when doing analysis, opening up numerous possibilities for novel kinds of analysis. The analysis by source of hire enabled RBC to emphasize different components of the employee value proposition when communicating to different groups. For example, campus recruiting efforts included networking events to provide interaction with existing employees, while postacquisition integration communications promoted RBC career-management resources and RBC's commitment to professional development.

RBC has also spent considerable time looking at the data to glean insights about managers and how that affects EOS measures. They looked at variables like tenure in the role and in the organization and rated performance to see if they could determine patterns to guide HR programs or other business interventions.

While HR cuts the EOS data by classical segments such as identifying what women say that is different from men's responses, the goal is always to find *meaningful* differences and point those out to leaders. For example, in the wealth-management division, men and women did have different perceptions about things like enablement and sufficient flexibility to support personal or family needs. HR brought that to the attention of leadership because leaders know how much wealth is controlled by women and believe a positive environment for women employees supports the bank's ability to be successful in that market. HR always looks for the patterns that are meaningful. They will not report, "Women said this and men said that" or "Gen Y employees said this and Boomer employees said that" unless the information connects to a business issue leaders care about.

HR gets constant feedback reinforcing the value of the EOS to the business. At one point when the survey was deferred by eighteen months because of an organization-wide change initiative, leaders came to HR asking for the survey: "We need the data!" Another indicator of success is the degree to which skeptics have been won over. In one business, the response rate was about 30 percent and the feeling there was that they were all so immersed in the financial markets that they did not have a lot of time for "HR stuff." Now, four or five years later, the response rate is over 70 percent because the connections between employee attitudes and business issues have been shown, and leaders have come to understand the EOS is not an HR program but a tool that provides them insights to run the business.

HR has also invested a lot of effort in proving that inferences drawn from the survey data stand up to scrutiny. For example, when people answer the survey saying they don't intend to stay with the organization, do they in fact leave? HR was able to do the analysis and show that it was a true predictor of voluntary attrition. Or when branch employees say they feel the bank has competitive products and services, does that really matter? RBC has concluded that answer is "yes" because the more strongly that employees feel the bank is competitive, the stronger the customer loyalty scores of those branches. Something like whether or not the bank has a high-interest savings account might not seem to have anything to do with HR, but at RBC it does—because they can see how a product like that influences employee attitudes and behaviors and from there how it ultimately affects outcomes with customers.

Building an Analytical Capability

What's the best approach to creating the analytical capability that can do this sort of EOS work: Make or buy? For RBC, the answer is both. RBC is a big enough organization and sufficiently committed to HR that they built an excellent in-house department, but they still make the most of external partners. They feel there is always something to learn and that working with their consulting partners is the best way to achieve that.

It is clear RBC never framed the question, "Which is cheaper, to use consultants or bring it in-house?" Instead, the question was how to get the most useful insights from data, and that naturally evolved to a mixed model with both strong in-house capabilities and strong partnerships with consultants. Survey design is a partnership, with HR bringing the strategic context and consultants, content options. Survey delivery is done by the consultant while HR handles all survey communications content. HR determines what analyses are needed following the survey with the consultant completing the analyses.

Underpinning the whole analytical project is a restless intellectual curiosity. They are not looking for the quick hit or headline-winning data point. They are patient in working to see what they can learn from the data and then dedicated to following through and taking actions that will make a difference for the organization and their customers. RBC uses the EOS the same way a biologist might use a microscope—it's the instrument that lets them see the mechanisms behind how employees drive business success.

Integration and Employee Commitment

With RBC we have seen how two major HR initiatives, diversity and EOS, are not merely HR programs but themes that run through the entire business. Within HR as well there is a constant emphasis on integration and alignment.

"It's more impactful if your recruitment strategy, your training, your performance and talent assessments, and your rewards are linked," explained Hirji. "It's more complex for HR for sure, but you are holding that complexity within a small group of people, and ultimately that helps the managers."

One of the tools that aid integration within HR is an overarching framework that focuses the different HR specialties on their long-term common objectives. Consistent use of this framework over a number of years helped change the mind-set and break down the silos so that, for example, a recruitment specialist would know not to run off and do her own thing in isolation; it all has to come together. "When we do talent assessments in the talent-management process," Hirji says, "the people involved are required to have thought about how the assessment will be used in performance, how it will be used in compensation and so on. That way, we don't end up with several incompatible approaches to assessment. People know it's the approach we expect, and a big part of my role is to make sure initiatives are integrated within HR, and that what HR does is integrated with the business." In simple terms, RBC consolidated similar but distinct assessments for performance, compensation, and long-term potential—that happened at different times—into a single assessment process at midyear that is revisited at year's end.

At first glimpse this requirement to connect all the dots looks like the opposite of the Nike slogan "Just do it." But RBC's approach is subtle. They want projects to move quickly, and they want everything to be integrated; it is up to staff to find the right balance between those potentially conflicting directives. Even if someone decides they do need to "just do it," the integration mind-set is there and they understand the cost of the trade-off in favoring speed over synergy. Fortunately, often it is possible to reconcile speed and synergy by looking ahead and being aware of and knowledgeable about the touchpoints. In practice this can mean taking a "test and learn" approach. When one division had a need for a new executive onboarding approach, HR moved quickly, followed some core principles about onboarding to ensure forward compatibility, and designed a new program. Afterward, with the benefit of lessons learned in implementation, the new program was relatively easily revised and integrated into the wider organizational talent framework.

That RBC is able to get employees at all levels to put in the extra effort to keep things integrated is a testament to the relationship they have with their employees. A big part of that relationship is founded on the bank's aim for employees to have long-term careers with RBC. They do not favor an employment deal where they hire someone for something they need at the moment, and when that is done the person is gone. Yes, it is a performance-based culture, and people are expected to perform well and develop, but as long as that happens, RBC wants to keep them over the long haul. This is good for the bank in that the workforce becomes knowledgeable and committed and, over time, will develop an effective web of business relationships within and outside the bank. It means that IT's innovation team will proactively reach out to connect with HR to share their latest on social media, for example, and find out where HR sees opportunity. HR in return is willing to support and lend its expertise to the IT-sponsored Student Innovator contest. Employees see the value of these sorts of cohesive activities to both their own success and company performance.

The long-term view shows up in employee attitudes. During the financial crisis, employee engagement increased, including employee willingness to work beyond what is required in the job to help RBC succeed, even though employee opinion scores in more personal areas, such as reward and recognition, declined. The long-term perspective benefits the workforce as well, and the call for performance and development is not heavy-handed. Employees want to perform well, develop, and succeed. RBC enables a good, long career for employees, and the employees enable long-term business success for RBC.

RBC is not the place to look for neat tricks or quick fixes. They have worked hard for many years to create the leadership, culture, and values that make synergy possible. HR intermeshes with their business partners as they create value for employees, shareholders, and customers alike.

Economics and Diversity

PROFILE

"My very first presentation in this role was to the diversity leadership committee," says Craig Wright, chief economist at RBC.

It might seem unusual for economists to place diversity so high on their agenda, but it is expected at RBC, where diversity is a business priority. The economics group has the tools and perspective to provide useful insights around diversity for the bank and for public policy.

"We did a big study in 2005 to raise awareness of the opportunity costs of not fully integrating immigrants into the economy," Wright explains. "Our leaders still frequently refer to that report today, as do government agencies and community groups."

That study put more rigor into the demographic analysis of diversity in Canada. People talk about different segments of the workforce in terms of ethnicity, gender, national origin, and sexual orientation; but add up all the numbers habitually tossed around and it ends up over 100 percent. The economics study gave everyone more solid numbers to work from.

The most dramatic part of the study was an estimate of the costs of not fully utilizing the skills of newcomers. Canada is highly successful at attracting immigrants—but not always successful at integrating them into the workforce. The study showed that if immigrants had work commensurate with their skills and education, it would add about $13 billion to personal incomes in Canada. The study also showed if women had the same labor market opportunities available to them as men, personal incomes would be $168 billion higher each year. These numbers back the case that diversity and inclusion are not just nice things to do; there is a large opportunity cost in doing nothing.

But who should do something? Too often a research group will identify a problem and then sit back and expect the government to fix it. RBC's view is that all levels of government have a role, businesses have a role, there is a role for professional associations, and there are things RBC itself needs to contribute. When responsibility is shared, there is more cohesion around change. At RBC, insights like these led to targeted recruitment programs that partner with immigrant employment-services groups, and the creation of an internal employee resource group that supports newcomers to Canada.

Seeing issues as pervasive rather than confined to silos is characteristic of RBC's thinking. "Diversity as a business issue reminds me of risk," Wright says. "In other organizations, the risk people are the police. They say yes and no. For us it is always risk and reward at every level. People who do deals always have an eye on the risk level, and the decision is based on both risk and reward. Diversity is the same way—people keep an eye on diversity at all levels, not just in HR. Everyone thinks about it on a regular basis."

Risk can be an important part of the diversity conversation, too. In position staffing, RBC has placed diversity candidates where there is great potential for long-term organizational benefit, despite some short-term performance risk, and has mitigated that risk by making temporary changes to job responsibilities.

Another characteristic of RBC thinking is to keep a long-term focus on common objectives. "Sometimes people feel there will be conflict where good public policy may not be good for the bank,"

Wright says, "but our belief is that if it's good public policy, it's good for the economy. And if it's good for the economy, it's good for the bank. Diversity is an example of where socially it's the right thing to do, economically it's the right thing to do, and it's the right thing to do for the business."

The 2005 research was not a one-off project. The economics group continues its work on diversity and frequently gives presentations within the bank, as well as to outside groups, and will continue to support the bank's commitment to diversity and inclusion.

Evidence-Based Change at RBC: Lessons Learned

RBC shows the power of connecting HR data, such as engagement and employee surveys, to business success, because it helps leaders understand the value and contribution of HR. However, for evidence-based change, it is the depth and specificity of the connection, not just showing the connection that makes the real difference. By carefully connecting the logic of RBC's strategy (helpful bank for a diverse and increasingly multicultural clientele) to the logic of RBC's HR investments (crafting programs that synergistically create both demographic and cultural diversity and empower the workforce to deliver diversity-focused outcomes), RBC literally changed how its leaders understand diversity. It created a leadership mind-set and behavior pattern that blur the line between HR and business strategy.

The power of diversity-based logic and analytics in creating synergy and optimization within HR, and between HR and the larger organization, has driven tangible change in behavior, mind-set, and results. Business leaders see EOS results as vital to their business decisions, in ways that were rare only a short time ago. They actually request more HR surveys and analysis, having learned the value of the information and how to use it.

Principle	Lessons
Logic-Driven Analytics	The fundamental approach at RBC—creating a plan for sustainable success first, and then supporting it with HR investments—provides a guiding logic that naturally creates a partnership built around HR's unique perspective on business success, rather than a model exclusively based on compliance or service delivery upon request.
	This can be seen in the example of diversity, where analytics and data are designed to show how ethnically diverse the workforce is, and whether the culture reflects values and beliefs consistent with diversity. When the organization simultaneously sees diversity in its customer base and services as a strategic imperative, savvy HR leaders can use that logic base to define how they will measure workforce diversity and connect it to the logic models that leaders use to define customer service.
	The Diversity 2.0 project shows the power of understanding that the necessary logic and analytics may lie in disciplines beyond HR. The HR group could have approached this workforce project through the HR logic of diversity and ethnic representation but instead opted to provide funding to the organization's marketing experts, engage them, and apply their analytical methods and data approaches (such as focus groups and segmentation) in ways that would blend the marketing and HR approaches to diversity.
Segmentation	Segmentation in marketing can be quite multidimensional, but in HR it is often based only on broad workforce characteristics (for example, high-potential employees versus others, or people who work in one unit versus those who work in another). RBC shows the power of taking a page from marketing, when they segmented the EOS data on two dimensions—the business unit (capital markets versus wealth management) and gender (women versus men), discovering that the interaction between the differences in the business units and the gender differences could reveal opportunities for optimizing investments in improving the employee value proposition.

(Continued)

Principle	*Lessons*
Integration and Synergy	RBC's business understanding—that the organization's success depends in part on serving diverse groups of customers—creates a natural opportunity for HR and business leaders to integrate the effects of workforce diversity on the services provided to diverse customers. The synergy between the business goal and the workforce goal is apparent, particularly where RBC's employees interact with customers. At a basic level, this synergy is illustrated by the fact that the workforce needs skills in fourteen languages in order to serve a customer base of great linguistic variety.
	This also means there is synergy between a culture of inclusion (an outcome of having built the organization on a diverse human capital base) and the way the organization approaches the challenges that come with serving customers that might at first seem "different."
	Diversity provides a high-level vision but also a specific and measurable outcome for employees and customers alike that reveals how branding, community, and employment investments can all work together. Diversity means that initiatives focused on employees, communities, and clients work together so that the totality is more than the sum of its parts. Avoiding bias in recruiting by delaying the revelation of data about where applicants earned their degrees, increases the possibility that more diverse candidates will advance. This in turn creates an image in the community of a bank that values diversity and creates community initiatives that are more effective and more credible, in keeping with the goal of helping newcomers, who in turn will want to work for RBC, an organization that they can see is dedicated to a diverse community and clientele.

RBC commits to the payoff from the synergy between HR programs more generally, and the organization's experience demonstrates that although integrating across HR functions is complex, complexity is held within a small group of people—a lesson for HR organizations that may find RBC's approach too complex. This approach may be as simple as ensuring that the people who design talent assessments for succession planning also confer and work with the people who will use the assessment data for performance management and rewards. This approach is closely intertwined with a culture that values long-term careers, so that when an employee makes a sacrifice today in order to serve the larger goal of integration, that employee is reasonably sure (although there is no guarantee) of being around long enough to benefit from a future sacrifice by someone else.

Optimization

The synergy between RBC's focus on diversity as a strategic goal and RBC's focus on diversity as a workforce goal leads to optimization. When there are hundreds of opportunities to do charitable work on behalf of the community, optimal choices can be made to foster the advancement of newcomers, to promote the inclusion of people of diverse backgrounds in schools and communities, and to encourage and support pride in the advancement of newly immigrated groups. Further, this focus contributes to optimizing RBC's future labor markets because it enhances skill levels and deep community commitment among precisely those people who will be the most attractive future RBC employees.

7

COCA-COLA COMBINES PASSION AND RIGOR

As the world's best-known brand, Coca-Cola needs no introduction. The Coca-Cola Company has operations in over 200 countries—more countries than in the United Nations. It is easy to imagine such a large, geographically dispersed human resources organization becoming a mass of well-intentioned but disconnected programs and policies.

However, Coca-Cola has managed to integrate its HR efforts to create synergies and avoid duplication. The global human resources team combines passion for their work with analytical rigor while focusing on enhancing the value of the enterprise in advancing its business objectives.

This case study explores how Coca-Cola's HR team starts with the company's long-term vision and strategy, partnering with business owners to set priorities and ensure alignment and integration at the local level. The end result is a series of talent development, succession planning, diversity, and capability-building initiatives focused on driving sustainable growth.

Integration with Clear Strategic Frameworks

The starting point for Coca-Cola as a business is their *2020 Vision*. Developed in partnership with several Coca-Cola bottlers around the world, this one-page roadmap outlines six goals (Figure 7.1) and then drills down into priorities, core capabilities, and metrics.

"At Coca-Cola, everyone knows the *2020 Vision* framework— every business unit and country and bottler. They all know

Figure 7.1 Goals from Coca-Cola's *2020 Vision Roadmap*

Profit: Double system revenue + increase margins

People: Be a great place to work

Portfolio: Be No. 1 in every non-alcoholic, ready-to-drink market

Partners: Preferred beverage partner

Planet: Global industry leadership in sustainability

Productivity: Manage for greatest effectiveness

how what they do aligns with the *2020 Vision Roadmap*. If they are doing something outside of the framework, then the question is why," said Terry Hildebrand, Global Director of Talent Management and Development, Coca-Cola.

The true test of any strategic framework is whether people use it—and, in the case of Coca-Cola, they do. This is a testament to the simplicity of the vision and the way it has been communicated to employees. "Clarity, simplicity, and consistency are three characteristics of our chairman Muhtar Kent," Hildebrand said. "He doesn't waver."

To get from the *2020 Vision* to the People Strategy, HR examined current changes taking place around the world, partnering with business leaders and teams from strategic planning and marketing insights to assess trends that will impact the business going forward. This meant going beyond traditional workplace trends and exploring those impacting the core capabilities of the business and driving profitable business growth (consumer marketing, customer and commercial leadership, and franchise leadership).

They also looked at key internal changes. For Coca-Cola, the biggest internal change has been the recent acquisition of Coca-Cola Enterprises' North American bottling operations, which boosted the company's total number of employees from 95,000 to 135,000.

The HR team was challenged with developing insights into how all the changes will shape how the company works in the future, how the workplace will be defined, what types of leaders will be needed, and how they should be developed. They also partnered with the business to look at the impact on building capabilities for both today and tomorrow.

This work allowed Coca-Cola to create its People Strategy, which, like the *2020 Vision*, is a simple, one-page framework consisting of four parts (Figure 7.2). Each of these four parts is supported by a detailed strategy. The picture of success entails communicating these strategies to the business in simple language (HR's elevator pitch) everyone can easily understand.

"It's straightforward on purpose," explains Ceree Eberly, Coca-Cola's chief human resources officer. "Everyone looks at it and says, 'Of course!' And they understand how the strategies behind the framework tie to the business. This is powerful because it is being brought to life in the business."

This type of framework functions in much the same way as a mnemonic. Journalists recite the maxim of "the five Ws and

Figure 7.2 Coca-Cola's People Strategy

Our People Strategy: 2011–2013

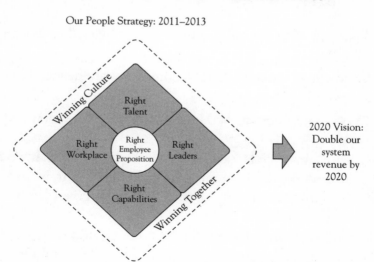

one H—who, what, where, when, why, and how—not because it writes the story for them but because it keeps them on track." A simple, usable framework like Coca-Cola's helps keep a global, diverse HR community focused on strategic objectives that deliver results to the business and not merely on individual programs.

Data-Driven Diversity

When Coca-Cola looked at the external world through the Right Leader lens, certain facts stood out:

- 70 percent of global household purchases are influenced by women.
- $20 trillion of spending is controlled by women, larger than the economic impact of the United States, China, and India combined.
- 40 percent of the global workforce is women.

That kind of clout makes the scarcity of women in leadership roles all the more striking:

- 3 percent of *Fortune* 500 companies are headed by women (2009).
- 6 percent of the top 100 tech companies are headed by women (2010).
- 15 percent of *Fortune* 500 board members are women (2009).

These data convinced Coca-Cola's business leaders that women were an underutilized source of leadership talent who could add a valuable viewpoint to their business, given their consumer base.

"I looked at who was buying our products and found that 70 percent of our shoppers were women," says CEO Muhtar Kent.

"Then I looked at our workforce—our senior team, middle management, new recruits, and our bottling partners—and saw a huge mismatch." This led to the creation of several programs to attract, retain, and develop women leaders including the global Women's Leadership Council, established by Kent himself. "We know we have a long way to go, but the numbers are getting better," says Kent.

HR does not end the story here. Like other data-driven companies, they track the ratio of women in higher grade levels to show that their objectives are being achieved.

The chain of logic is to start with the data, view it through the lens of a future forward strategy, ensure initiatives are coordinated, support the needs of the business, and then measure progress. The work at Coca-Cola is not about a passionate diversity department looking for new things to do but a passionate HR team partnered with the business to create the right leadership talent needed to reach the company's goals—which, in this case, meant developing women leaders.

Integration Without Squashing Flexibility

Strategy at Coca-Cola is not seen as senior leadership dictating a one-size-fits-all operating model. Coca-Cola believes decisions must be made as close to the business as possible. They look at key talent from a global perspective while providing "freedom within a framework." Everyone knows they must focus on the right talent, but most decisions within that global framework are made at the local level.

The process of finding the "Right Talent" varies by country. For example, China is such a high-growth market that everyone is trying to hire the same people. In addition to a shortage of professional workers who can operate within a global context (who are fluent in Chinese and English), Coca-Cola's business success is also linked to the shortage of manufacturing workers. In China, Coca-Cola pursues initiatives targeting the manufacturing segment—a unique issue for them, but one that flows from the framework outlined in the global People Strategy.

In other countries, hiring good logistics people is projected to be a serious challenge because Coca-Cola's customers want them, their competitors want them, and other industries want them, too. In those countries, acquiring the right talent means developing programs that are specifically targeted at the needs of this pivotal role. Every part of the business thinks about talent, but within their own context. The Right Talent framework drives discussion with HR and the business that is essentially about segmentation, first identifying critical segments and then taking targeted actions that make sense for each country.

The Right Capabilities lens operates in a similar way in getting HR functions around the world to ask the right questions to determine what is most critical to the business in their respective markets in both the short and long term. In India, this lens highlights the need to enhance the skills of retail professionals; sales data show rapid growth of Coca-Cola's products in this market, so India is a clear investment priority.

What is interesting about Coca-Cola's approach to India is that HR partnered with business leaders to identify the right capabilities needed for their system and the retail industry as a whole (Figure 7.3). By examining the bigger picture, HR set out to create a series of strong programs that extended beyond the company's walls.

One such initiative is the Coca-Cola Retail Academy, developed in partnership with Coca-Cola bottlers, local institutions, and other companies with a stake in the retail industry. A second capability-building initiative is Coca-Cola's University on Wheels (CCU-on-Wheels), a bus-turned-mobile classroom that seats twenty-two people and is used to train retailers, distributors, and sales representatives. CCU-on-Wheels travels around India providing education to help modernize India's retail industry.

CCU-on-Wheels delivers two programs: Parivartan (which means "change" in Hindi), which equips traditional retailers to

Figure 7.3 Coca-Cola's Capability Requirements in India

We will need to build capabilities for our system as well as develop capabilities for the industry

KEY SYSTEM PRIORITIES	Coca-Cola	Industry
	CURRENT PEOPLE PROGRAMS	
Franchise capability development	✓	
Innovation	✓	
Commercial and customer leadership	✓	✓
Supply chain	✓	✓
Route to market	✓	✓

succeed in India's evolving modern retail format, and Advanced Parivartan, which covers ROI, credit cards, value-added tax, customer footfalls, promotion management, and people management.

Mr. Pappu, who runs the Jai Durga Store in Agra, said, "The most important thing I learned from Parivartan is stock management and dealing with customers. I learned how to order, how much to order, and how to deal with different types of customers. My daily sales have increased from IRs2,000/- to IRs3,500/-."

Mr. O.M. Prakash, of Shri Ram Daily Needs in the Punjab, cited environmental gains as well as bottom-line gains. "We implemented the learnings from the Parivartan program by switching from plastic bags to eco-friendly biodegradable bags. As a result, our sales have increased by approximately 10 percent to 15 percent."

To date, over 55,000 participants have received training through these programs in more than eight hundred small towns across the subcontinent. This initiative, which started with one bus, now has a fleet of three buses. Coca-Cola is currently collaborating with its bottlers to invest in additional buses.

"With the tremendous growth in the retail space, we need to build the capability for successful retail management.

Our initiative is not about how to sell our products better, it's about the co-creation of skill sets. This innovative practice, the first of its kind, is being driven by our Human Resources function in collaboration with our bottling partners," adds Atul Singh, president, India and South West Asia.

Corporate-led educational initiatives in the developing world can look like simple community service projects. Yet for Coca-Cola, the consistent application of their People Strategy framework leads HR in different countries to partner effectively with the business to determine what type of investment is needed to yield best results for the business, their customers, and their consumers.

Integration of Core HR Processes

If we look back to the People Strategy in Figure 7.2, we don't see a "box" for core HR processes like rewards, performance management, or development. The Strategy diagram reminds HR professionals that these individual processes are integrated across these four strategies to provide a more holistic approach to driving business results.

One example of integration is the emphasis on rewarding potential *and* performance. Like many organizations, Coca-Cola insists on differentiated rewards, with short-term rewards focused on performance. However, from a succession-management point of view, key talent is critical. Therefore, if scarce reward dollars are being allocated, then it makes sense to also reward potential. At Coca-Cola, this is done mainly through long-term rewards. To make this all work, extensive calibration exercises are conducted to ensure fairness and consistency in decision making. Calibration sessions often fall by the wayside in many organizations because they call for a rigorous and often time-consuming process of aligning manager perceptions and perspectives. Yet any organization that really wants to have a credible and effective reward system must invest in this kind of effort.

Coca-Cola's desire to differentiate rewards based on potential as well as performance does not imply an "up or out" culture. While the bar on performance is continually raised and everyone is encouraged to develop and grow, Coca-Cola sees value in having some people spend longer periods of time in certain global roles that require strong depth and breadth of experience in the Coca-Cola system. There are also numerous opportunities for talent to take on shorter, more developmental assignments as part of their overall portfolio of experience, which are rewarded and reinforced across the globe.

Coca-Cola's People Development Forums (PDFs) also align with the reward and performance-management processes. PDFs are a management routine Coca-Cola has institutionalized to ensure they have the talent needed to execute their business strategies for the short and long term. During this process, managers identify key talent, conduct succession and development planning, and look at moving talent both internally and across the system (between the bottlers and Coca-Cola) as well as identifying key leadership capability needs for the future and how to build them.

While this is a compensation-driven administrative process at many companies, at Coca-Cola it is an important ongoing routine for business leaders. Approximately 85 percent of leaders are engaged in this dialogue at least quarterly, and senior leadership of the company formally discusses people during their monthly meetings. Information from the performance-management system feeds into the process, including individual performance, development needs and desires, mobility preferences, and career aspirations. So development conversations are not removed from conversations about rewards and performance; it is simply another venue for managers to continue their conversation about people.

The fact that Coca-Cola has institutionalized these practices over the last few years has led to measurable improvements in how they manage and deploy talent. These include increasing the tenure of senior leaders in current roles (from 20 percent with at least three years to almost 50 percent). The business has

Figure 7.4 Coca-Cola's People Development Forum (PDF) for Review of People Development by Function and Business Unit

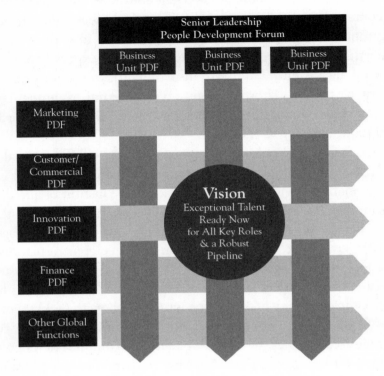

defined this measure of success because building capability and sustainability in key markets is important for the longer-term business growth and health of the company. Other key improvements include an increase in the ability to fill roles internally (up to 85 percent from 75 percent) and an improved ability to deploy talent across groups.

Another example of HR seeking synergy and helping the business was bringing external talent acquisition of front-facing roles in-house. The thinking behind this was based on these metrics:

- For the best search firms, up to 40 percent of the talent Coca-Cola is interested in is off limits because of agreements the search firm has with other companies regarding "poaching" staff.

- Candidates hired by search firms turn over 2.5 times more often than candidates recruited by HR working directly with the business.·
- The average time to fill a vacancy is 30 percent longer when the recruitment is handled by a search firm than when it is done in-house.

A broader objective is creating a deep talent pipeline encompassing both internal and external talent. With the clear connection to external as well as internal talent, Coca-Cola can manage their pipeline in a more integrated way and stay connected with the marketplace.

Integration Through Culture

While one can readily point to tangible integration elements at Coca-Cola, such as a common strategic framework or a common technology, something more intangible is also helping to drive integration—their culture.

Culture starts with the business leaders, who expect to see holistic HR solutions to business issues. They don't want to see training, diversity, and performance management developing disparate, siloed programs.

In addition to affecting how HR creates or communicates solutions, it can also impact structure. For example, the talent-management function has been combined with talent development to create a totally integrated approach based on requests from business leaders who didn't want to have a conversation about talent needs one day and another on learning and development the next. They wanted an integrated conversation, and HR's solution was to combine the two.

"We all know the business requires us to provide integrated solutions. If you come in with a siloed approach, then you're not doing your job," said Terry Hildebrand. "There needs to be synergy."

Passion

This case study began by noting that passion is vital to the Coca-Cola culture, starting with employees and extending to customers and consumers. For HR, this passion means supporting the business by developing scalable programs rooted in strategy.

"We have a business to run, so knowing that HR is there to truly partner with us to find real-world solutions—versus coming up with new training or benefits solutions—is wonderful," said Doug Jackson, Business Unit President, Greater China and Korea. "They have a passion for what they do and a passion for our brands and our business. It's a great combination, and together we are working to achieve our *2020 Vision* goals."

Eberly added, "For us in HR, this is a journey. We've made some important gains, but we still have work to do. We just need to stay focused and work diligently to provide the business with the global and local solutions needed for the short and long term."

Evidence-Based Change at Coca-Cola: Lessons Learned

Coca-Cola is a forward-looking organization that has integrated its HR efforts with a level of consistency and rigor globally. These ingredients, combined with a universal passion for one of the world's greatest brands, help Coca-Cola create and ensure a common focus on what is important to its business, regardless of an employee's geographic location or function.

Cultivating a focused, inspired culture is hard work, however. It requires repetition, reinforcement, and discipline. This comes from a mind-set of evidence-based change focused on the business.

Coca-Cola uses evidence-based change as a critical tool for driving consistency and rigor in its decision making and creating alignment around its core strategic frameworks. As this case study demonstrates, Coca-Cola's approach to evidence-based change focuses on an integrated view of the entire talent life cycle in addressing a given business issue (integration and synergy) and considering the role of distinct segments of the workforce in realizing the *2020 Vision* (segmentation). The ability to continually ask the question, "How will this help us achieve the *2020 Vision?*" is at the heart of this approach.

Principle	Lessons
Segmentation	As we have discussed before, there are two sides to the issue of segmentation—the demand side and the supply side. Coca-Cola presents interesting examples of both.
	The ability to recognize and meet the needs of specific pivotal roles as Coca-Cola did in both India with its CCU-on-Wheels program that targeted traditional retailers and China with its focus on manufacturing and logistics staff, is a classic example of demand-side segmentation.
	Similarly, the focus on women, while a very large segment, is a great example of supply-side segmentation. The organization recognized the unique needs of women and the business value the organization would gain from this focus. Coca-Cola developed a holistic plan, including processes in talent acquisition, development, and rewards. These key processes were linked to a key strategic talent objective around how the organization managed its succession-management and talent-deployment processes to ensure a robust pipeline of highly qualified female talent. This is a classic example of leveraging the entire life cycle to bring about a systemic solution to the needs of a particular segment.
Integration and Synergy	Integration and synergy are evident in two core areas.

(Continued)

Principle	Lessons
	First, they are apparent in how HR partnered with the business to complete a robust, integrated look at both internal changes and global external trends to assess the impact on the core capabilities of the business and its ability to drive profitable growth. This meant going beyond traditional HR trends to incorporate consumer, customer, and overall marketplace trends.
	Second, integration and synergy are evident in how the organization aggressively leverages all aspects of the talent life cycle to build capability and address various business challenges. But this not only focuses on connecting the various talent life cycle elements so they are not in conflict, it also is about using logic to dictate which elements should be emphasized where and when. Whether it is sourcing talent in China, developing retail capability in India, or grooming the next generation of women leaders, Coca-Cola continually looks for connections across all aspects of the talent life cycle.
	Consider the organization's People Development Forums. While many might not consider it a revolutionary approach, its power lies in Coca-Cola's ability to use this management routine to link all key components of talent and development. The framework (Figure 7.4) illustrates the flexibility the organization has created by integrating both a geographical and global functional review to ensure they have the talent needed to execute their business strategies for the short and long term.
	Coca-Cola recognizes that building a high-performance culture requires well-sourced and qualified talent (consider its decision to insource recruiting) who have the flexibility to grow and thrive in a variety of roles and situations.

8

KHAZANAH NASIONAL'S PURSUIT OF NATION BUILDING

Can evidence-based change play a role in nation building? Khazanah Nasional Berhad is certainly doing its best to prove it can. Khazanah is the strategic investment arm of the Malaysian government. It has stakes in over fifty businesses in a wide range of strategically important industries, including telecommunications, transportation, utilities, and infrastructure. The mission of Khazanah is not merely to invest in these businesses but to help enhance shareholder value creation and the performance of the companies in a way that will ultimately benefit the whole nation.

Malaysia might have a lower profile than its Southeast Asian neighbors of Thailand and Singapore, but it is one of the world's great success stories. Malaysia is a multiracial democratic country that has gone from being a poor, largely rural British colony to being a thriving nation with a solid middle class and a diversified economy.

The government has long played an active role in guiding the nation forward. Khazanah serves the government's long-term vision by supporting development of organizations that can grow to be regional or even global champions. In May 2004, the Government-Linked Companies (GLCs) Transformation Programme was launched, under the patronage of the Putrajaya Committee for GLC High Performance, with a series of initiatives across all GLCs, such as one to enhance board effectiveness, another to revamp procurement practices, and one on optimizing capital management.

An initiative of special interest to us is the Orange Book initiative, whose objective is to strengthen leadership development in Malaysia. The initiative extends beyond the companies Khazanah invests in, thanks to the support of other government-linked investment companies, such as the Employees' Provident Fund, the Lembaga Tabung Haji, the Lembaga Tabung Angkatan Tentera, and Permodalan Nasional Berhad, which also have investments in a wide range of companies. As a result, twenty companies are participating in the Orange Book initiative, nine of which are owned by Khazanah. In addition to these private-sector organizations, various government departments have joined the initiative.

The underlying belief is that by working together, the organizations can do better at developing leaders with the different skill sets required for alternative business conditions than any one could do on its own. Furthermore, there is a point at which leadership becomes a national resource. If companies can grow great leaders, that will be a benefit to Malaysia, even if some spill outside the network of government-linked companies into other parts of the economy.

How do you go about improving leadership development on such a broad scale? The industries are very different, and each company needs to be allowed to run its own business. Khazanah does not want to impose programs so much as bring the participating companies along on the journey to higher effectiveness. In this chapter, we focus on two major parts of the Orange Book initiative:

- Help companies improve by getting them involved in "doing and feeling" leadership development, including a cross-organization leadership exchange
- Introduce a leadership development audit to help companies understand the status quo and set a baseline

Doing and Feeling Leadership Development

Encouraging better leadership development included promoting proven approaches, such as external coaching, a mentoring program, and formal coursework. However, Khazanah also had a radical idea in the back of their minds. Surely there should be some way to get synergy from the group of companies. Couldn't leadership development in the portfolio be more than the sum of its parts? Khazanah had an idea: why not transfer people between companies as a way to accelerate their development?

The beating heart of this notion is widespread recognition among leadership development professionals that the best learning comes from challenging assignments. The trouble any one organization faces is that there are not enough challenging assignments to go around. But consider how much someone from a senior role in automotive might learn from a stint in an airline or what an experience it would be for a leader from a stable utility to be thrust into a management role in the world of high tech. By facilitating a leader exchange, Khazanah could have a huge impact on the development of high-potential leaders in Malaysia.

An IMD case about the Orange Book initiative quotes Malaysia Airlines CEO Dato' Sri Idris Jala: "If we accelerate the development of employee talent through an exchange program, they can reach their maximum capabilities by 40 years of age due to the experience they gather—as compared to reaching it close to retirement age. This way, they can work for 20 years at their full potential." And yet, as the CEOs and HR vice presidents of the companies met with staff from Khazanah, some real-world problems arose. The important thing to remember is that Khazanah is an investor, not a group that manages the individual companies. Why would one company or government department give up a star leader so he or she could work somewhere else? Did it even make sense to place a leader in a developmental assignment in a dramatically different industry? What if the pay structure of the new company was different from the one the star leader had come from? Would the receiving company really trust an unknown person in a position of authority?

These potential problems were numerous, but the group forged ahead. To corral the problems into a manageable shape, Khazanah's companies came up with a set of ground rules:

Talent Pool

- The talent would be high-potential middle managers capable of senior executive roles.

Assignments

- A project-specific role would last six months to one year.
- A full role would last one to two years.

Conditions

- There would be no poaching; the talent would return to the originating company.
- The role would have to include a developmental focus and/or mentoring.
- The home company would pay the talent's salary and bonuses.

However, while the companies could agree on those ground rules, it was not at all obvious how the actual matching of person to job would be done. Would CEOs meet and swap people? Would the high-potential people participating in the program go out and pick the jobs they wanted from a list? In the end, Khazanah was asked to broker the process for the first round. It was not a role they relished as it gave them more direct control than they felt was appropriate, but this was the best way to get the program going.

Khazanah did insist that any participating organizations both give and receive talent. However, they were not overly strict on auditing who went into the program. If the organization thought the person would benefit, that was enough. Khazanah did not want to pressure organizations on which leaders participated until the organizations had learned to trust the program.

Successes, Problems, and Lessons

The initial success was that the exchange took place, driven not by the authority of a head office but by a common conviction of the participating CEOs that this would be good for the individuals, good for the company, and good for the country. The success of getting the program off the ground was soon muted by a number of initial problems. Some people didn't like their new jobs, some felt they lacked the authority to make an impact, some were unhappy about the benefits, and some wanted to drop out. Rather than interpreting these issues as a sign the program wasn't going well, the problems were treated as a kind of diagnostic, identifying issues that would be addressed in the next round.

It became clear that to make a good decision about the match between a job and a candidate, the candidate had to have a lot more information about the job. In the second round, the matching was done much the same way jobs are normally filled. Candidates chosen by their companies to participate in the program were shown the list of jobs available, and they interviewed for the ones they were interested in. This resulted both in better matches and clearer expectations. What was unusual is that instead of a finance person going to a finance job, there might be a finance person going to a marketing job based on the specific skills he or she brought to the position. The program encouraged participating companies to think broadly and look for breakthrough opportunities—to try things they might not normally have considered.

Another lesson learned from the first round is that people moving to a new role needed specific types of support. According to Shahnaz Al-Sadat Abdul Mohsein, Khazanah's executive director of strategic human capital management, "Many people had the initial expectation that when you have very good talent, you can put them anywhere and they will immediately thrive.

That notion came crashing down in the first few weeks. There is always a significant feeling of discomfort as soon as someone moves out from their own company. No matter how good the talent or how good the match, people have this unsettling experience when they arrive in a new organization."

Khazanah organized meetings among the cohort of managers involved in the program so they could network, learn from each other, and also benefit from a sense of community. Additionally, the cohort had meetings with CEOs—not just the CEOs of their own companies but also those from other participating organizations. These are intimate meetings, and both CEOs and the managers learn a lot about each other and leadership development in general.

Finally, every two months the chief secretary of the Government of Malaysia speaks with the managers in the program who are working in government departments. They have conversations about what leadership looks like and what they have learned. This conversation is one that has proven exciting to the managers and helps reinforce that they are part of a program that has importance to the nation, not just their own careers.

One measure of success that Khazanah tracks is what becomes of the people after they return to their home company. The results so far are very good, with a high percentage rapidly being promoted to more senior roles. A broader measure of success is simply the number and quality of people sent on the program. Companies have seen the value of the exchange and don't need to be talked into giving up top-caliber talent for a couple of years because they now recognize the value of the development that takes place.

Leadership Development Audit

In addition to the leadership exchange and forums/communities, there was a third significant element in the Orange Book initiative: the Leadership Development Audit. The goal was to provide good information about the gap in leadership and the quality of the leadership development programs in Khazanah's group of companies. A company might think, "We've got a good leadership development program" or "We're happy with how we develop leaders." But what is that opinion based on? If they don't have experience with talent development in other companies, how would they know what an excellent program looked like? The audit would provide hard data so that companies could make informed decisions about whether the programs were good enough, as well as being a diagnostic that showed which aspects of the program could most be improved. Everyone might agree that a particular aspect of a program was very important, but if the audit showed it was already being well done, then the question arises as to whether further investment in that aspect would yield a return.

There were two main elements to the audit. One was to look at the projected leadership gap; the second was to look at the quality of the processes meant to close the gap.

The Leadership Gap

Determining the leadership gap was a matter of looking at the number of current leadership positions and then stepping down to the number of leaders available in three years by projecting attrition through retirement, turnover, inadequate performance, and so on. The demand side of the equation comes from projecting the need for specific types of leadership to handle new projects and company growth. The distance between supply and demand is the leadership gap. Figure 8.1 shows the graphic used to illustrate the gap.

This is a relatively simple approach and does not need to be highly accurate to be very useful. It serves to focus management's attention and gives them a handle on the scope of the problem. What the participating organizations found was that the leadership gap was very large. Individually and collectively they would be far short of the numbers of hard-driving leaders they needed in their growing economy. This lit a fire under the CEOs to commit to filling the gap.

Figure 8.1 Sizing the Leadership Gap

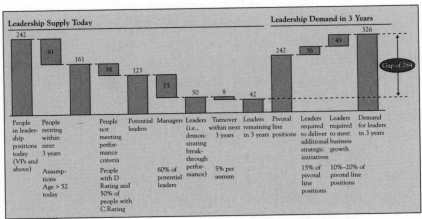

WHY THIS METRIC IS USEFUL
This metric enables the Company to identify the number of leaders required to deliver the company's KPIs and to meet the growth plan. The size of the gap will determine how much focus needs to be given to both "buying" and "building" leadership talent.

Another useful output of the current-state analysis was an organization chart showing an assessment of current talent with red, yellow, and green coding identifying low-potential, high-potential, and gold-standard incumbents (Figure 8.2). This simple chart moved attention from the overall talent numbers to specific key positions. As with the leadership gap assessment, this provides a tool participating companies might not have previously used to focus discussion on something concrete. It provides a tool managers can use to talk about leadership development using common measures of leadership potential and readiness to advance.

Another tool the audit introduced was an analysis of overall progress made in developing leadership competencies (Figure 8.3). Organizations that had leadership competency models would use this analysis to get a picture of whether, overall, their bench strength of leadership talent was improving. Organizations without a leadership model (eight of the 20) realized they needed one. The message from the audit was that you must have a model, you must measure progress, and you must have an action plan to improve. While each organization would

Figure 8.2 Testing That Pivotal Positions Are Filled by Top Talent

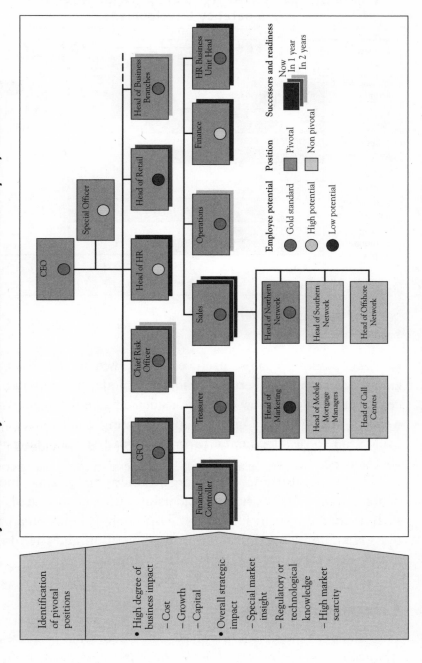

Figure 8.3 Sample Analysis of Aggregate Progress in Competency Development

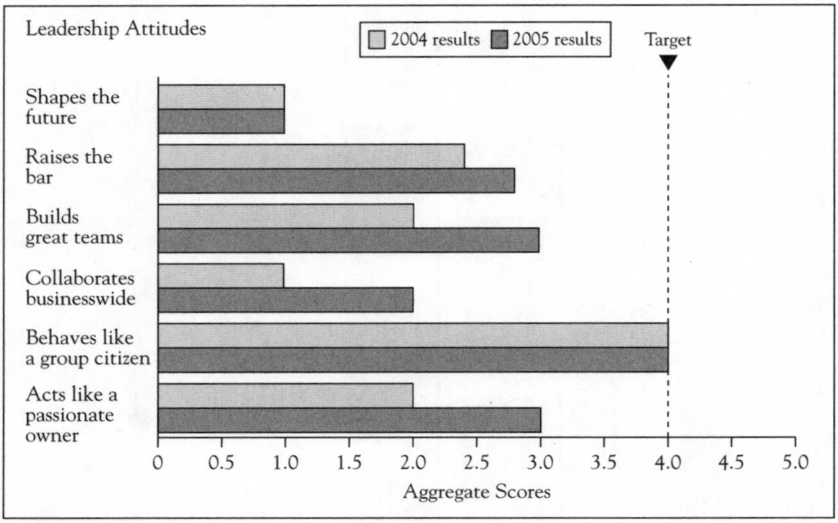

Note: Reviews of top 250 leadership groups

Source: Employee opinion surveys.

be benchmarking against itself, using its own model, there is enough commonality between leadership models that Khazanah could get an overall view of where leadership competencies were weak or strong in the group of participating companies. This could lead to developmental programs aimed at addressing the common weaknesses.

The audit also encourages organizations to become more deliberate in how they handle leadership turnover with analyses such as that shown in Figure 8.4. This analysis helps organizations separate planned from unplanned attrition and then look at the reasons behind the unplanned attrition.

Assessing Processes

The audit of processes involved an interesting two-stream approach. One stream was to look at the perceptions of those in

Figure 8.4 Turnover Analysis

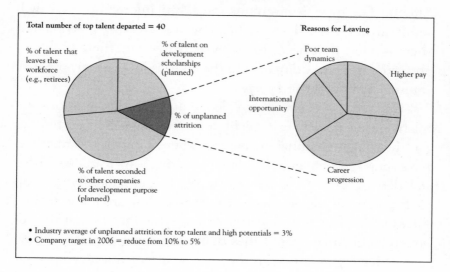

Total number of top talent departed = 40

% of talent that leaves the workforce (e.g., retirees)

% of talent on development scholarships (planned)

% of unplanned attrition

% of talent seconded to other companies for development purpose (planned)

Reasons for Leaving

Poor team dynamics

Higher pay

International opportunity

Career progression

• Industry average of unplanned attrition for top talent and high potentials = 3%
• Company target in 2006 = reduce from 10% to 5%

the leadership pool themselves about how good the talent development processes were. The other set of data, the hard data, involved looking at the talent development processes themselves: Were they in place? Were they effective?

Both streams of data are valuable, and organizations found it of interest to compare the two. The hard data are not necessarily more accurate than perceptions, and having both explicitly laid out set the stage for serious discussion about which aspects of leadership development were strong and which were weak. The value of the processes audit is that it set the stage for an informed decision about which processes should be improved to best close the leadership gap.

Continual Progress

For all the Khazanah initiatives there is a long-term perspective, with the conviction that with every cycle the process will get better. As of 2010, Khazanah was on the third round of the Leadership Development Audit, and one of the changes is that they are increasingly referring to it as a review rather than an "audit." The focus is always on providing information that will result in improved decision making, not creating a sense that there is a test that needs to be passed. However, there is also an appetite for increased rigor, and the audit is increasingly done by internal audit or a third party.

The process has also revealed that some organizations are relatively talent-rich and might not have enough opportunities for their high-potential managers, whereas other organizations have shortages of talent. They are pondering ways to address these imbalances, and while no one wants to permanently give up high potentials, leaders recognize that if they are going to lose talented employees, it is better to keep them in the network of government-linked companies than have them go outside. The idea of letting talent go so they can soar is still a new idea but is very much talked about. Treating leadership as a national resource is a work in progress, and participating organizations are building a solid foundation for what they intend to be a very tall structure.

Another area of lively discussion is the difference between leaders inside a government-linked company versus those in the purely private sector. One differentiating competency that has been identified is political savvy, and a module to address that is being added to the program. Over time, the discussion of leadership competencies is likely to lead to more commonality in leadership development models, which will further enable integration and synergy.

Khazanah's Orange Book initiative has got a large group of organizations in Malaysia engaged in being more deliberate and analytical about leadership development. The organizations are working together, thanks to forums and communities, shared concepts, common methods, and even an exchange of talent. It serves the government's long-term goal to bring Malaysia fully up to the level of the most economically advanced nations.

From Private to Public Sector

In 2009, Aqtar Fariq Syahril Othman, a manager at Malaysia's well-regarded electricity company Tenaga Nasional Berhad, took a leap into government as part of the Orange Book leadership-exchange initiative.

"I have had five different portfolios in the last ten years because I like new challenges," says Aqtar, "so this exchange appealed to me."

Aqtar's new role was in the Malaysia Administrative Modernization and Management Planning Unit (MAMPU). MAMPU has a mandate to spearhead the transformation of the public sector through improved management and information technology. Aqtar might have been excited to dive into the unfamiliar world of government, but that did not make it easy.

"It was tough at first," he recalls. "I was in a high grade, and the expectations were high. I struggled to adapt to the culture and work style."

The transformation work itself was a natural extension of what had been his most recent post at Tenaga, where he had worked on productivity and quality management. Still, Aqtar needed to prove he could achieve results inside the public sector.

"It took three months, but I managed to convince my colleagues in MAMPU that I could excel in that environment," Aqtar says. "You have to be patient and learn to adapt to gain their respect. Also, you have to stay passionate about your work."

MAMPU gained a good manager for the year Aqtar worked there. His skills in consulting, change management, and public speaking all proved valuable. In addition, Aqtar gained a whole new appreciation for government.

"The government has changed a lot, actually," he says. "It's not like the 1980s era. They are forward-looking, efficient, and working to transform."

In fact, Aqtar fell in love with the work MAMPU was doing, but Tenaga needed him, and when his year was up, he was pulled back to Tenaga, where he has taken on a role in HR.

The experience was clearly of great value to Aqtar. He was exposed to new kinds of challenges, developed his network outside Tenaga, and learned to understand how the government works and to appreciate the good work it does. He would not have been able to find such a fresh developmental challenge if he had stayed inside the familiar world of Tenaga. He also developed some specific expertise in business-process reengineering as well as a sophisticated methodology for collaborative problem solving.

MAMPU had the chance to benefit from the specific work that Aqtar did. But, more than that, his peers there had a chance to see the approach and mind-set of a manager from the private sector.

Tenaga is benefiting as Aqtar finds that the skills he developed in MAMPU are of value in his new work. The sessions with leaders from the government and government-linked companies changed his way of thinking, and he feels that he is a better manager now and is ready to lead a small business.

One can imagine sending a manager off to an executive MBA program, but it is unlikely that Tenaga could have found any classroom experience that would have had as deep and long-lasting an impact on Aqtar as his year with the government did.

Into the Deep End

After a series of assessments and performance reviews, Che' Mohamad Izmi Bin Ibrahim was nominated by his company to participate in Khazanah's cross-company exchange program. He immediately accepted the chance to test his abilities in a new environment. It proved to be a turning point in his development as a leader.

Che' Mohamad Izmi had worked for fifteen years at Celcom Transmission (M) Sdn. Bhd., a Malaysian telecommunications company. He had done well and had a comfortable career. That comfort evaporated as the exchange program sent him to Malaysia Airlines (MAS), the flagship national airline. Not only was he entering a completely different industry, the job Che' Mohamad Izmi moved into at MAS was also unlike anything he had done before. He landed in the program-management office, managing a wide range of IT projects across the company. Although he had a strong technical background, he had never been involved in program management, and it was like learning to swim by being thrown into the deep end of the pool.

"The first three months were a challenge for me," Che' Mohamad Izmi says. "I had to learn program management, learn the processes, become familiar with the organization, get to know the project owners, and identify the issues. It was all new and difficult. I wondered if I'd be able to do the work. But my supervisor and colleagues were very supportive, and it turned out that the technical skills I'd brought from Celcom were valuable at MAS."

The supportive environment at MAS was important in making the exchange successful. Che' Mohamad Izmi also benefited from the work done by the secretary of the exchange program, who organized monthly events, such as meetings with CEOs from government-linked companies. Che' Mohamad Izmi was swimming in the deep end, but he had good coaches.

After his exciting year at MAS, Che' Mohamad Izmi returned to Celcom, where he had a new corporate role and a new perspective as a leader.

"The program really helped me a lot," he says. "It changed my mind about what I can do as a leader. I now know what I am capable of. I'm also a better manager. I spend more time doing one-to-one coaching to develop people."

Organizations need resilient leaders who can take their organizations into new markets or launch new technologies. The future is uncertain, and the value of adaptive leaders is unquestionably high. On its own, Celcom would not have been able to replicate the kind of thrown-into-the-deep-end development experience that Che' Mohamad Izmi had at MAS. Two very different companies found that by working together they could enhance the development of the nation's leaders.

Evidence-Based Change at Khazanah Nasional: Lessons Learned

Khazanah is a great example of applying a number of our principles to address issues on a national scale. It clearly illustrates the power of leveraging multiple diverse entities to develop a leadership talent pool equipped to deal with a myriad of business models, challenges, and cultures.

Khazanah uses evidence-based change as a critical tool for engaging its various stakeholders (companies, other governmental agencies, and so on) in pursuit of its overall goal of nation building. Evidence comes in many forms, and the right evidence to drive change may often not be the most sophisticated numbers, statistics, or hypotheses. The case illustrates how some basic analytics around the emerging gap in leadership talent were combined with a common vision of what was needed for the success of the nation.

Principle	Lessons
Logic-Driven Analytics	Analytics is often synonymous with numbers, statistics, scorecards, and mathematics. This case shows that this kind of rigor and depth is appropriate and useful in HR. Khazanah has conditioned its companies and stakeholders well to view data and analytics as critical requirements for any change. Its various colored books have provided both a fact base and a roadmap for bringing about change in multiple areas, from board effectiveness to strategy to procurement and leadership development. Each of these books cleverly relates global best practices to what is important and needed in the Malaysian context. For example, the Orange Book audited the projected leadership gap and the quality of the processes that were meant to close this gap (relative to global best practices). This then led to the establishment of the leadership exchange, coupled with ongoing measurement and the involvement of various CEOs and government leaders to ensure that change was measurable and sustainable.

The audit established some logical frameworks for assessing the leadership gap through the use of a set of leadership competencies; a formula for calculating attrition; a straightforward graphic for illustrating inflows, outflows, and gaps in leadership; and a "stoplight" scorecard to show where problems might exist.

Risk Leverage The approach encourages considering talent risks, both within and across organizations, with respect to providing some unique dilemmas and opportunities. As the case illustrates, a basic requirement for the system to work was that organizations were willing to take risks by giving up their talent to other organizations, when that talent might not return or when the development experience might not be effective. The Khazanah system and governance structure strove to strike the right risk balance by avoiding being too strict about the standards of the experience, or about requirements for the talent to return, and yet by not being so hands-off that there was a risk of chaos. Organizations are encouraged to take risks that have the potential for high payoffs in terms of skill diversity and the creation of a national leadership resource. The Khazanah systems of auditing, scorecarding, sharing best practices, and overseeing the exchange process are all examples of a unique system for achieving cross-organization risk optimization.

Integration and Synergy The leveraging of multiple companies and governmental agencies to develop the leadership talent pool for the country is a great example of integration and synergy. The group of organizations was able to advance faster in leadership development than they could have on their own. By establishing a standard audit for assessing leadership development processes, each participating organization was able to improve its programs. By creating opportunities for the organizations to share ideas about leadership development, they accelerated learning. Finally, by exchanging high potentials between organizations, they found much higher-impact developmental assignments than any companies could have arranged in-house.

(Continued)

Principle	Lessons

The gains from synergy and integration are realized at four levels:

- *National level*. The nation now has a large pool of talent that has been developed for multiple business and economic models by virtue of the unique developmental experiences that each participating organization is able to provide.

- *Company level*. Each organization now has leaders who have gained experiences that were not available within the company. Those leaders in turn will provide the organization with a very different perspective than might have been possible in the past and thus more effectively challenge the status quo. (Consider the discussion in Chapter Three about the value of hiring someone who will say, "Turn left" when everyone else is saying, "Turn right.")

- *Individual level*. Individuals will acquire unique skills and broaden their own leadership capabilities. (Consider the example of Aqtar Fariq Syahril Othman of Tenaga Nasional, who moved into a governmental agency. He was able to acquire skills and perspectives that were not available at Tenaga and thus increased his value to his current employer as well as to any future employer.)

- *HR level (functional areas)*. The common infrastructure discussed earlier has become an integrating mechanism for how talent is sourced, developed, and rewarded across the participating companies.

Optimization

The existing system has achieved the important goals of engagement and acceptance across organizations, and a common framework for tracking progress. With these important foundations in place, there is a basis to enhance optimization as well.

One can foresee that as the system identifies gaps, the priority for leadership development exchanges might be shifted to emphasize movements that would address those particular gaps. The system orchestrated by Khazanah could be particularly powerful in providing a cross-organization perspective.

Organizations might mistakenly conclude there was no need to develop certain competencies if they individually projected having enough for their own uses. Nevertheless, the optimal solution for the Malaysian talent base might be for the collective group to build those competencies anyway if other organizations have shortages, or if the collective national need is quite high. Organizations with enough or more than enough of one competency might be encouraged to develop other competencies through the exchange process, in return for the opportunity to use the exchanges to build those competencies that are more scarce for them.

9

IBM'S WORKFORCE MANAGEMENT INITIATIVE

IBM is an interesting organization because it went from a period of total dominance of its industry to near bankruptcy to a revival as the leading global provider of technology solutions. The abrupt changes of fortune have left IBM a forward-looking company that is anything but complacent. To stay ahead of the curve, the company has pioneered effective approaches to optimizing the deployment and development of talent globally.

The IBM story starts with CEO Sam Palmisano's awareness that globalization was changing the nature of business. Trade and investment flows across national boundaries had liberalized, protectionism was falling, and technological advances had vastly reduced the cost of global communications and business computing, leading to shared business standards throughout much of the world. This changed the idea of what was possible through globalization:

> Together, new perceptions of the permissible and the possible have deepened the process of corporate globalization by shifting its focus from products to production—from what things companies choose to make to how they choose to make them, from what services

---

This case was published by the Society for Human Resource Management (SHRM ©2010) in collaboration with the National Academy of Human Resources. Copies of the case, parts A, B, and C, are available on SHRM's Web site at www.shrm.org/education/hreducation/pages/cases.aspx.

they offer to how they choose to deliver them. Simply put, the emerging globally integrated enterprise is a company that fashions its strategy, its management, and its operations in pursuit of a new goal: the integration of production and value delivery worldwide. State borders define less and less the boundaries of corporate thinking or practice [Palmisano, 2006].

Palmisano coined the phrase *globally integrated enterprise* to describe what he had in mind. He foresaw that IBM's clients would increasingly be moving toward global integration and that IBM needed to get ahead of that trend. This had implications for every aspect of IBM, including significant implications for IBM's supply chain, IT systems, strategy, marketing, and services development and deployment. Underlying all these implications were significant challenges for IBM's human capital and its approach to human resource management.

Human Capital and Globally Integrated Enterprise

Of course, talent and human capital were becoming increasingly vital to competitive success in all organizations, but they offered an even greater strategic pivot point for IBM. IBM competed mostly on its ability to deliver unique know-how and practical solutions to clients, rather than on a particular hardware or software product. The knowledge, motivation, skill, and deployment of IBM's workforce were even more vital than for many of its competitors. In 2003, IBM had approximately 350,000 employees. IBM employees were highly qualified and motivated, but the existing workforce systems simply could not provide the global flexibility that would be needed to serve the needs of IBM's evolving clients.

The customer was saying, "Know my business and provide value propositions that are unique to me." Yet while IBM sales and service experts were highly skilled on IBM products and solutions, increasingly it would be their unique knowledge about the client's industry and global implications that would be key differentiators. Furthermore, although Palmisano envisaged IBM as a globally integrated enterprise, IBM's workforce systems often operated within the boundaries of countries or regions— projecting demand and providing supply for their country or region but without any global integration.

The key for future success lay in developing the ability to move talent quickly between countries, whether physically or virtually. IBM needed to be able to quickly and accurately find the capabilities of its workforce, wherever those capabilities existed, and deploy them against clients' problems faster and at a lower cost point than their competition.

Furthermore, consistently low utilization rates had plagued a portion of IBM's business for some time. A utilization rate is the ratio of billable hours over available hours. The total nonutilized time shows the value that could be tapped if the workforce were more consistently doing billable work. IBM's utilization rates had been below industry standards and below IBM's own targets for many years. It would have been tempting to design a simple initiative that would specifically target utilization rates, perhaps by holding business leaders accountable for achieving industry-standard levels, or by identifying individuals "on the bench" waiting for assignments and providing stronger incentives to deploy them to projects.

While such a system would likely bring utilization rates more in line with industry standards, it would not achieve the more significant goals of truly integrating the elements of talent supply and demand and helping leaders make better decisions about employee development and deployment.

IBM's talent-management systems were state of the art by any standard and yet seemed inadequate to serve the talent needs of a globally integrated enterprise. What was the fundamental limitation in the current systems? Randy McDonald, senior vice president of HR, and his team realized the very language of the work might be at fault. At first glance, you might think the solution to the dilemma of managing talent globally would not be difficult. You might think that you could generate the talent development and movement you needed by just requiring managers to contact their counterparts when they had needs or surpluses. Leaders in France could ask leaders in the United Kingdom or Germany, or vice versa. Yet, as the HR leadership team considered what would happen when such contacts occurred, they realized the language used to describe the work in different countries, professions, and even different projects was like comparing apples and oranges. This is one reason that employee movement so often hinged on whom the employees knew and on making the right personal connection. Just like most other organizations, in IBM direct personal knowledge was often the only practical way two opportunities in different countries could be compared. The managers would have to sit down and hash out in detail what they meant by things like work tasks, qualifications, key success factors, and so on. What was missing was a common language.

Many organizations have adopted skills inventories or competency-based systems that do provide a kind of common language. However, such systems are usually applied either in very technical areas, where skill sets are easily defined, or with leadership development, where broad competencies like "vision," "flexibility," and "ability to execute" can be used. The challenge IBM faced in developing a common language was that if it was too specific, it would not provide much more integration than the myriad work descriptions IBM already had. On the other hand, if made too generic, it would fail to capture important nuances.

The Workforce Management Initiative

Some kind of expertise taxonomy would have to provide the common language for global talent management, but that would have to sit within a broader system called IBM's Workforce Management Initiative (WMI). Here is how IBM described it:

> WMI addresses the labor-based business issue of managing resources effectively and seamlessly across business units and geographic borders. This is accomplished through an integrated set of processes and supporting tools designed and deployed to make IBM's workforce management effective, efficient, and competitive.

At its core, WMI is a series of strategies, policies, processes, and tools that enable optimal labor deployment, built on a foundation of learning. IBM believes workforce optimization requires linkages of four key disciplines:

1. *Resource management* requires accurate inventory of skills and talent, demand forecast, capacity planning, and workforce rebalancing.
2. *Talent and mobility* requires a common taxonomy, common profiles for all sources of labor, and decision support.
3. *Learning* requires tight alignment with business objectives, accurate skills assessments, skills-gap management, and alignment with skills development systems and programs.
4. *Supplier or vendor management* requires alignment of supplier strategy with resource-management strategy.

To communicate the rationale for the new approach, IBM created a one-page diagram showing why WMI was put in place (Figure 9.1).

Figure 9.2 shows how IBM's HR and executive team envisioned the future of IBM's On Demand Workplace. A core idea was that the underlying database would be comprehensive, supporting decisions about talent mobility, vendor management, learning, and resource management. Another core concept was borrowed from operations management—the idea of an integrated

Figure 9.1 Why the Workforce Management Initiative (WMI) Was Put in Place

1. IBM had:
- No design for end-to-end resource-supply chain
- No central accountability for workforce management

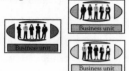

WMI brings:
- Common supply-chain design based on best practices
- Central oversight of measurements and investments

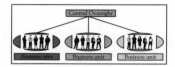

2. IBM had:
- No standard for defining the workforce
- Labor pools managed independently by business units

With WMI:
- Workforce is consistently cataloged across business units (*Expertise Taxonomy*)
- Labor supply pools are optimized at the country level

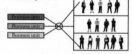

3. IBM had:
- Limited forecasting of anticipated resource demand
- Difficulty in linking training investments with market needs

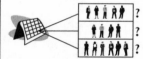

WMI is working toward:
- Resource forecasts using one common language (*Expertise Taxonomy*)
- Training investments driven by forecasted shortages

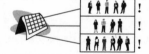

4. IBM had:
- No unified sourcing strategy
- Management systems that did not encourage cross-unit collaboration

WMI processes, policies, and tooling bring:
- Optimal use of resources
- Alternate work models
- An increase in variable labor mix

> WMI is a series of strategies, policies, processes, and tools that enable optimal labor deployment built on a foundation of learning.

talent-supply chain. The result would be a talent-management system that would operate more like a continuously adapting supply system, rather than simply a repository of information about jobs or skills.

Figure 9.2 The Workforce Management Initiative (WMI)

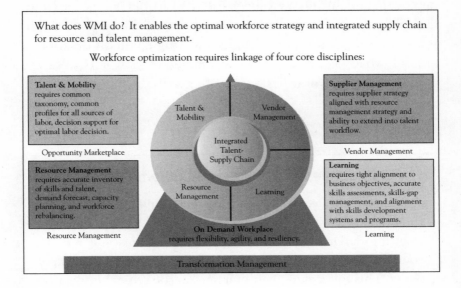

What does WMI do? It enables the optimal workforce strategy and integrated supply chain for resource and talent management.

Workforce optimization requires linkage of four core disciplines:

Talent & Mobility requires common taxonomy, common profiles for all sources of labor, decision support for optimal labor decision.

Opportunity Marketplace

Resource Management requires accurate inventory of skills and talent, demand forecast, capacity planning, and workforce rebalancing.

Resource Management

Supplier Management requires supplier strategy aligned with resource management strategy and ability to extend into talent workflow.

Vendor Management

Learning requires tight alignment to business objectives, accurate skills assessments, skills-gap management, and alignment with skills development systems and programs.

Learning

Talent & Mobility

Vendor Management

Integrated Talent-Supply Chain

Resource Management

Learning

On Demand Workplace requires flexibility, agility, and resiliency.

Transformation Management

To make this a reality IBM had to:

- Establish and implement a common language to describe IBM's talent resources—the IBM *Expertise Taxonomy*
- Develop an optimum workforce management strategy linked to the business strategy, using the language of the taxonomy
- Capture an inventory of all talent resources in a central data store
- Create the capability to operationally match resource supply against demand (capacity planning) and proactively identify excesses and shortages—linked directly to business strategy

The *Expertise Taxonomy*

The *Expertise Taxonomy* is the hierarchical framework that IBM uses as a standardized, enterprisewide language and structure.

This language is essential to IBM's ability to plan, develop, and deploy its talent resources consistently across all geographies and business units. The taxonomy identifies things such as job roles, job role skill sets, and skills, creating common descriptors around what people do. (Two examples of how job roles are described are shown in "Examples of *Expertise Taxonomy* Roles.")

Examples of *Expertise Taxonomy* Roles

Application architect: This role designs applications required to automate business processes and meet business needs. The resulting design may run on multiple platforms and may be composed of multiple software packages and custom components. This role defines best practices in the critical evaluation and selection and/or development of the software components and hardware requirements of the applications and data, and in the development of the application, including evaluation and selection of development methods, development processes, best practices, and tools. Application architects are responsible for applications-related quality, performance, availability, scalability, and integrity. They are also responsible for the functional interface to applications and for ensuring application usability.

Procurement consultant: This role is responsible for analyzing client category spend data and developing category-specific sourcing and risk-management plans. This position supports the sales and solutions teams with extensive category expertise and interfaces with the client on the category-specific strategic sourcing objectives. Additional responsibilities include the execution of contract requirements related to the assigned category as well as reporting to the project and procurement leadership team on status, issues, and corrective actions.

The taxonomy would support up-skilling programs that would enable employees to compare their existing skills to various job roles and identify skills needed for another role. The program would seamlessly integrate this skill inventory function with the capacity to enable employees to identify and apply for open positions in the company's job posting system. When employees identified an open job they were interested in, the system would show them what learning activities would make them more "marketable" for such a position, in the shortest time.

IBM business units would be able to use the taxonomy to optimize their operations. For example, IBM Global Business Services would use job roles and job role skill sets to deploy their employees to appropriate contracts and positions based on the skills listed in client contracts and project descriptions. IBM Global Technology Services (GTS) would use the taxonomy in their Go-to-Market model for their Face-to-Face sales team. The taxonomy would provide consistent and comparable role definitions, job role skill sets, and incentive plan templates across all four GTS lines of business. This was important because the frontline sellers in each of the four lines of business were supported by skilled technical resources that spanned the business units, residing centrally in GTS Sales/Delivery or other business units. Prior to the taxonomy, the Go-to-Market model was too complex, and it was difficult or impossible to appropriately match sales roles to presales technical support roles. With the taxonomy, there would be only seven standardized sales roles and three presales technical support roles that align GTS with other IBM business units. The GTS Go-to-Market model would have clear and concise roles and responsibilities for opportunity identification, opportunity ownership, and delivery.

A Peek at Implementation

A good example of how even a simple idea requires sophisticated resolution in a global talent system is the notion that there should be one global job application process. What that means is that whenever someone applies for a job at IBM, across the globe, the information provided will be consistent and readily uploaded into the talent taxonomy system. The issue of globalization was paramount. Although IBM could find vendors who could create an application system in a given country or region, no vendor had the global scale to create and oversee an applicant system worldwide on the scale of IBM's employee population. Yet if IBM did not have a global standard for applicants, a significant element of the talent supply would become invisible to the system.

Ted Hoff, IBM's chief learning officer, noted, "We had to cobble together the vendors to create a global recruitment event in our system. The world really wasn't ready for the idea. Issues such as global privacy, information sharing, language compatibility, and so on suddenly needed to be resolved. The idea that every IBM applicant would submit information in a similar way, and that the information would immediately be available across the company, seemed logical but actually flew in the face of some long-standing global traditions. For example, Germany places an additional set of privacy restrictions on the way information can be collected or shared within IBM about individual applicants. The United States places additional requirements on reporting information to ensure there is no adverse impact on specific diversity groups among the applicants. The province of Quebec, Canada, requires that the actual text in IBM's global recruitment system, the Global Opportunity Marketplace, is written in French as well as English."

The rationale for a global system was compelling and the vision of WMI was clear, but it would be a mistake to underestimate the practical challenges of putting it all in place.

The Payoff

As noted earlier, one signal that the old workforce management system was not working well was the low utilization rates. Under the new system, IBM's calculations showed that the billable utilization rates improved nine percentage points between 2003 and 2008. WMI has lowered the number of people "on the bench" and improved fill rates to over 90 percent in global delivery. With the taxonomy, IBM could more precisely, efficiently, and effectively match upcoming supply and demand, allowing them to proactively manage future bench and open seats, thereby increasing utilization and reducing open seat conditions. One improves cost, the other improves revenue.

An HR leader related a specific case in point: "Hyperion [a database] is an area of focus for IBM right now, and frankly, in the past it has had a feast-then-famine demand signal. Putting those resources in one job role skill set has helped IBM closely manage its growth and follow a specific sourcing strategy: hire upper levels, hire some selective lower levels, and so on."

In short, the taxonomy and the system supporting it enabled IBM to smooth the "demand signals" coming from project and unit talent requests, and to respond in a far less costly way.

Another source of financial payoff came through the systems effects on optimizing the contractor workforce. IBM had tens of thousands of contractors in 2005. This was far fewer than the number of full-time employees, so the IBM leaders did not expect the financial payoff for contractors to be the source of such significant financial results. However, what became apparent as the system was implemented was that IBM had much greater knowledge and awareness of the status, capabilities, and deployment of its full-time employees than of its contractors. Although the full-time and applicant elements of the workforce came under the purview of HR, decisions about contractors were largely made by businesses or regions, often in response to significant short-term talent needs and often with much less input from HR.

As Frank Persico, the HR leader who oversaw the creation and management of the taxonomy, recalled, "Our full-time employees were reasonably well known. It was the contractor space that had the greatest potential. Contractors would be brought in on the belief they had the skills the supplier said they had, but in fact they often didn't. It wasn't that the suppliers were misleading us. Rather, it was that the language the suppliers used to define contractor capabilities didn't line up well with the language we used to define our business needs. So there was lots of room for improvement in the degree to which we actually matched contractor skills to their best possible use, and in making sure what we were paying them was actually commensurate with what they were doing. Just knowing which contractors were actually working while being paid was helpful. The operations could really clearly see how applying the taxonomy allowed us to rationalize what we paid contractors by having much greater insight into their skills, deployment, and value added."

The WMI system had indeed cost millions, but it paid for itself just in the hard savings from better contractor management, not counting the improvement in full-time employee management. Persico observed that the payoff equation was best understood through a financial-management lens, not an accounting lens: "We found that if leaders took an accounting approach, they would become fixated on the costs of the system, time spent working with it, and so on. However, if they reframed it into a financial investment question, then the value through better contractor and employee management was clearer, and it became clear that the large investment paid off."

Evidence-Based Change at IBM: Lessons Learned

Starting with a view of where the business was going, IBM realized it had to pioneer a new way of managing talent as a global resource. The underlying metaphor was that of a supply chain. There were various sources of talent (existing internal talent, internal talent that could be trained to do new things, and contractors) and various demands for talent (projects around the world). The trick was to match the deployment and development of supply in a way that matched forecast demand.

This clear, logical model was easy for stakeholders to understand but was by no means easy to implement. Supply chains of parts are simpler than supply chains of humans because parts are standard, whereas humans are not. Still, IBM persevered in creating an expertise taxonomy that was detailed enough without being too detailed and all the supporting systems to ensure talent could be identified, developed, and matched against demand.

For organizations interested in pursuing this kind of integration, the encouraging thing is that IBM was able to demonstrate a very clear payoff. Logical frameworks, optimization, and integration really do add value even when implementation is a complex process.

In the case of IBM, the evidence driving the change in talent management came from two very different directions. One was from the broadest level of strategic planning: recognition that IBM's clients were becoming globally integrated enterprises and would need a truly global solutions provider. The second piece of evidence was a key business metric: low consultant utilization rates. In addition to the hard numbers, IBM's HR leaders cited instances where making the right moves occurred only because of the happenstance that one leader knew another, and where opportunities were missed because the language of human capital differed across units.

The evidence provided the impetus to change; the specific solution of the Workforce Management Initiative required a bold leap and skilled implementation.

Principle	Lessons
Logic-Driven Analytics	HR's use of a well-understood business metaphor—the supply chain—as the basis for their global human capital planning meant that leaders throughout the organization could easily understand and engage with the goals and the approach.
	The IBM case illustrates how something as basic as defining work requirements can create a logical framework detailed enough to be useful and simple enough to be maintained. In the absence of this logical framework, the Workforce Management Initiative would have foundered. The logical need for such a language, and for everyone to cooperate in using it, was apparent through the supply-chain lens because a common language (for example, a stock-keeping unit, or SKU) is a fundamental supply-chain requirement.
Segmentation	IBM launched its global workforce initiative in the segment of its business that offers consulting and other services, where billable hours and utilization rates provided quantitative data for planning, design, and evaluation. In addition, this was an arena where talent supply was particularly responsive to clear information about development opportunities and project options.
Risk Leverage	As with a traditional supply-chain system for raw materials, in-process inventory, or unfinished goods, the IBM global workforce initiative created a system that better articulated risk and return. Understanding clearly how project demand and supply were related meant that IBM leaders could clearly see where taking early risks on talent development (creating an early recruitment presence in universities; producing skills that would be needed in the future, or in a country where demand would increase but a skill base would need to be built) was more feasible in light of the connections revealed by the system. Employees could better assess the personal risks and returns of decisions about which competencies and career paths to pursue. Based on information about where long-term project demands seemed to be increasing, they could more easily switch their paths as conditions were starting to change.

Integration and
Synergy

Integration and synergy do not come automatically in large organizations. IBM knew idle talent in one country might be desperately needed in another; however, matching demand to supply was impractical without a common language and common systems. Once a global workforce management system was built, each country could benefit from resources elsewhere in the IBM world.

At the same time, the tool for matching talent demand to talent supply also served to provide better information for career planning and skills development. Thus the system truly created a 1 + 1 = 3 situation, where better talent-deployment information clarified the available and most needed development opportunities. In this way, IBM created a better qualified workforce with more insight into employees' development.

An unexpected payoff of having an integrated system to describe talent was much better management of contractors, showing that integration produces important synergies that were not foreseen.

Optimization

The global workforce management system is also an exercise in optimization. Not only is the utilization of people optimized, development investment is focused on those areas where the projected demand is high and withdrawn from areas where the projected need is low. As in a traditional supply chain, the paths through which talent moves can be optimized against cost, time, and ultimate value, and investments can be made to enhance talent movement at the bottlenecks.

10

AMERIPRISE FINANCIAL REINVENTS ITS HR FUNCTION

In 2005 the leaders at Ameriprise Financial found themselves in interesting times. The organization had just been spun off from American Express. This gave them a great opportunity to drive the business to new heights of success, but it also meant grappling with the fact that they had suddenly lost a great deal of the infrastructure American Express had provided. For staff groups, big holes needed to be filled immediately. For HR, something as basic as payroll became a major issue. However, the HR function did something inspiring—they managed to see beyond the crush of urgent problems and used this time of transition to begin implementing a fresh vision of what HR can be.

Ameriprise's HR function used logic-driven analytics, segmentation, and optimization to create an evidence-based change journey that went from getting the basics right to becoming a key contributor to the strategies of Ameriprise's business leaders. Along the way, Ameriprise learned valuable leadership and operating lessons for any HR organization making this transformation.

Getting the HR Basics Right

Ameriprise has a long history. The business began in 1894 under the name Investors Syndicate. Then as now, its objective was to help people plan for and achieve their financial goals through a tailored approach and product solutions. Today the company has around eleven thousand employees and serves more than two million individual, business, and institutional clients. Yet, after the spin-off from American Express, it did not feel to HR that they were in an old established company, because they found themselves grappling with a host of serious and urgent issues.

Often spin-offs are handled gradually, with the new organization continuing to contract for services from the parent firm until the new organization gets all its systems in place. In the case of Ameriprise, the transition was abrupt. And this mattered to HR because American Express had a shared-service model. It was not just that HR had lost strategic elements, such as a reward strategy or talent-management processes. HR also needed to replace basic services American Express had provided, including payroll, benefits, a call center, and HRIS. HR did not even have everyday tools such as a template for an offer letter. Kelli Hunter, executive vice president of HR, describes those early days as being a time of "focusing on getting the basics right in HR."

Getting the basics right was hard work, and for a time it was difficult even to execute the basic transactional HR services. The case has been characterized as one of the largest in U.S. history and was executed in a short time frame—it was like being in an $8 billion start-up. Not only was HR called upon to build its own professional function from the ground up, this had to occur at the same time the Ameriprise business that HR supported was also rapidly adapting and needed extra help.

In the 2006 review of department performance, which included feedback from internal customers, HR got disappointing ratings. Hunter's internal customers were not getting their needs met, and she was committed to getting that rating up by getting the basics right. But getting core functions of HR running efficiently was not the end point of Hunter's vision. The challenge of being part of a billion-dollar start-up was something that attracted Hunter to the job. Here was a chance to build a business-minded HR function that focused on adding value, not just delivering services. It was an opportunity to create an organization where things like culture and values were understood not as a vague HR notion but as critical drivers of profitability. In 2005, when Hunter interviewed with the CEO, Jim Cracchiolo, she discovered they shared the same vision. Cracchiolo spoke in terms of employees as family. He wanted Ameriprise to have an HR function that would bring to life the principle that an organization needs engaged and results-focused people, and you get that through values and a mission people believe in. Hunter recalled Cracchiolo telling her that her colleagues on the executive team expect to achieve strong results through their people. They needed HR's help to see how to do that, and to identify if it's working for the business.

It was an exciting opportunity, but at times a challenging experience, to make big changes in the HR team's mind-set when it already had so much on its plate. Still, Hunter knew that it was not a question of whether she would pursue this vision but how.

Bringing Focus to the HR Function

It was also an emotional time for HR as they faced the dual challenge of getting the basic functions running again and learning the unfamiliar business-focused view of HR that Hunter was championing. Not only was the business-focused view of HR new to Ameriprise, it was uncommon in the industry. The existing model of HR delivery was based on responding to whatever internal customers might want, as well as introducing interesting new HR initiatives. For example, a manager might be concerned with turnover, so HR would redirect efforts to respond, or an HR leader in a business unit might discover an interesting mentoring technique at a conference, so they would implement it. There was no doubt a lot of good work was going on, but it was not directed by any consistent business logic. It was often reactive, and it was all on a transaction-by-transaction basis.

In 2005, this was typical of most HR functions that pursued a "program delivery" paradigm. Yet there was a big potential payoff to doing things differently. Hunter, and other forward-thinking HR leaders at the time, could see the potential in extending the paradigm with a greater focus on the strategic value added by HR. It would reduce extraneous work that was not adding value and set the stage for HR's becoming a real partner to the business rather than a responsive provider of services.

Hunter said, "We kept coming back to the theme of aligning HR with the business. We just kept hammering on that theme. We had to get the team to understand that they don't just show up for work. They must actually contribute to adding value. It was about going from being an order taker to being a proactive commercial partner."

Though this perspective is common today, in the financial services industry of 2005 it was a new idea for which there were few existing role models. What logical framework could capture the vision?

Hunter settled on a products-and-services model she had observed during her years working in consumer products at Mary Kay and the Gap, and at financial services companies like Morgan Stanley and Bankers Trust. In both the consumer product and financial services worlds, organizations operate on a fundamental logical model that includes a very clear focus on their products, measuring how each is doing, and retiring less popular products to free up resources for new ones that will better meet customer needs. HR does a great many things, but it was rare to think of these as a portfolio of products, and it was even rarer to think that the right approach is to measure the usefulness of these products to customers and kill off the low-return ones. The products-and-services model Ameriprise came up with for HR is illustrated in Figure 10.1.

This systemic view of HR may seem simple, but the HR team had grown up in a very decentralized structure, with relatively little integration. It was a significant task simply getting the HR team to list all the different things they did. The word *team* was even a new idea. The HR staff had never all been in a room together before 2005. As a result, it was a challenge for Ameriprise to get its arms around all the things HR did, but it

Figure 10.1 HR Products-and-Services Model

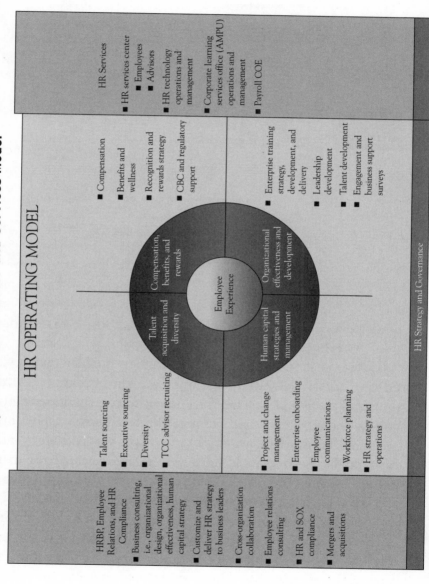

HR OPERATING MODEL

- Compensation
- Benefits and wellness
- Recognition and rewards strategy
- CBC and regulatory support

- Enterprise training strategy, development, and delivery
- Leadership development
- Talent development
- Engagement and business support surveys

HR Services

- HR services center
  - Employees
  - Advisors
- HR technology operations and management
- Corporate learning services office (AMPU) operations and management
- Payroll COE

- Talent sourcing
- Executive sourcing
- Diversity
- TCC advisor recruiting

- Project and change management
- Enterprise onboarding
- Employee communications
- Workforce planning
- HR strategy and operations

Circle diagram
- Talent acquisition and diversity
- Compensation, benefits, and rewards
- Employee Experience
- Human capital strategies and management
- Organizational effectiveness and development

HRBP, Employee Relations, and HR Compliance
- Business consulting, i.e., organizational design, organizational effectiveness, human capital strategy
- Customize and deliver HR strategy to business leaders
- Cross-organization collaboration
- Employee relations consulting
- HR and SOX compliance
- Mergers and acquisitions

HR Strategy and Governance

Figure 10.2 Linking HR Products and Services to Shareholder Value

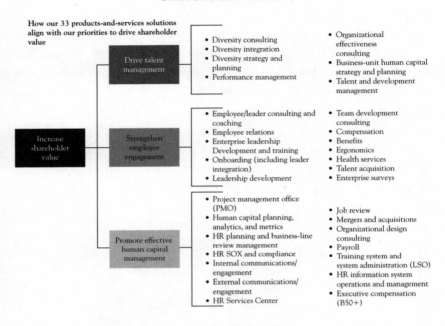

How our 33 products-and-services solutions align with our priorities to drive shareholder value

Increase shareholder value

Drive talent management
- Diversity consulting
- Diversity integration
- Diversity strategy and planning
- Performance management
- Organizational effectiveness consulting
- Business-unit human capital strategy and planning
- Talent and development management

Strengthen employee engagement
- Employee/leader consulting and coaching
- Employee relations
- Enterprise leadership Development and training
- Onboarding (including leader integration)
- Leadership development
- Team development consulting
- Compensation
- Benefits
- Ergonomics
- Health services
- Talent acquisition
- Enterprise surveys

Promote effective human capital management
- Project management office (PMO)
- Human capital planning, analytics, and metrics
- HR planning and business-line review management
- HR SOX and compliance
- Internal communications/ engagement
- External communications/ engagement
- HR Services Center
- Job review
- Mergers and acquisitions
- Organizational design consulting
- Payroll
- Training system and system administration (LSO)
- HR information system operations and management
- Executive compensation (B50+)

was a necessary first step in reframing HR's contributions around business value.

The next step was to determine how these products and services created shareholder value. That was done first by identifying three drivers of shareholder value: drive talent management, strengthen employee engagement, and promote effective human capital management. Then, as shown in Figure 10.2, it was possible to align each product/service to a value driver. This created the much needed linkage between the flurry of activities that kept HR busy and the value HR created for the business.

This framing of all the activity that went on in HR in terms of shareholder value set the stage for thinking in a disciplined way about each product/service and for each one assessing the quality, the efficiency, and how good the tools were.

"I used the metaphor of a grocery store," Hunter says. "Imagine someone is going into the frozen food aisle, looking for ice cream.

We should not be rushing around trying to provide strawberry swirl at the request of one particular customer when we don't even have vanilla and chocolate yet. We need to focus on the most important products that add the most value, and not do the rest."

This products-and-services model stressed two ideas. One was that all the products/services existed because they linked to HR drivers that increase shareholder value. The second idea was that there was a portfolio of products/services, and each one should be subject to scrutiny based on its effectiveness and how it worked with other products/services. Before something new was added to the mix, the question would be asked as to whether it added enough value to be on the list. Similarly, the question was raised as to which existing products/services needed to be removed or altered. The model provided a fundamentally different way of thinking about the HR function, one focused not on one initiative after the next but on a coherent strategy for adding value.

In the old model, the fact that an internal customer wanted something was essentially all the justification HR needed to deliver it. Ameriprise also introduced an idea from marketing—Kano analysis (Figure 10.3). Kano analysis plots how well a need is fulfilled versus customer satisfaction. It is not true that satisfaction always goes up in a linear way with how well a need is met. For example, with payroll, there is high dissatisfaction when the need is *not* fulfilled, but only moderate satisfaction when it *is* fulfilled. Products/services with this kind of profile are *musts*. If satisfaction goes up every time the product/service is improved, then that is a *want*. An example of a *want* is leaders' desire for opportunities to develop. The third kind of profile is where the customer does not really expect the product/service so if the *need* is not fulfilled, the customer will still be satisfied but if the product-service is provided, he or she will be delighted, hence the *delights* category. Mentorship could be an example of this category.

The value of this model is that it provides a logical framework for HR to organize its analysis and decision making to focus

Figure 10.3 Kano Model

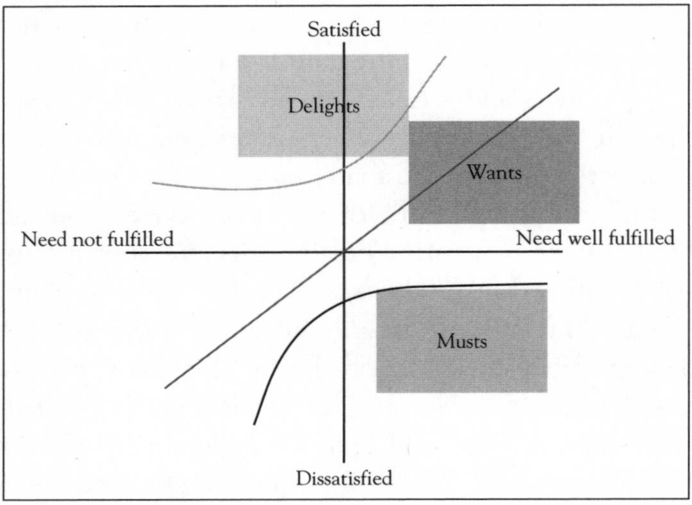

Source: Adapted from John W. Boudreau, *Retooling HR: Using Proven Business Tools to Make Better Decisions About Talent* (Boston: Harvard Business Press, 2010).

its efforts rather than simply responding to a client request or interesting opportunity. In an era where getting the basics right was an issue, HR had to focus a lot of attention on the *musts* (payroll, call center, and benefits) and think hard about whether other initiatives were *wants* or *delights*. The framework does not dictate answers. Ameriprise might decide to invest in some *delights*, but they would do so having thought about it in light of the Kano model. This was a particularly useful way to think through the complexity that existed in Ameriprise due to having a diverse population spread over many locations. This kind of thinking led to various changes, such as

- Retiring some training programs
- Eliminating certain reports
- Changing the way some training programs were delivered (for instance, using a more efficient Web-based delivery)

- Changing the delivery of the wellness programs
- Revamping the intern program
- Changing the campus recruiting process
- Retiring some of the things diversity was doing and enhancing others

An important process for ensuring this kind of disciplined thinking that was going on in HR was the business-line review (BLR). Every HR function would report back monthly on what they were doing to serve the business. This process kept the logical models in front of the HR team and continually brought them back to questions around what was adding value and what was not and if their customers were satisfied. Hunter notes, "We don't say no if a business wants something. Rather, we invite them to work through the problem with us and logically help us all decide what works best and makes the best contribution."

A Finance Expert Confronts HR

One way for HR to take advantage of the logical frameworks and points of view prevalent in other parts of the business is to bring in people with non-HR backgrounds. Hunter knew she needed a very strong leadership team to implement the transformation she desired. One of the new leaders was Penny Meier from the finance function, whom Hunter invited to be vice president of workforce planning and strategy in 2007.

Although Meier came from the finance function, it was not her finance skills per se that HR was seeking. It was business-mindedness, grounding in analytical rigor, and knowing how to deliver on goals. Meier's skills included expertise in business transformation—how to create the infrastructure to move a business forward and know that it is moving. Another was project management experience. One specific skill was investment optimization, and with Meier in HR there was a chance to apply the same kind of discipline in optimizing the investment in people that was applied to optimizing the investment in the program portfolio across the enterprise. Meier would arrive with an experienced eye toward seeing corporate functions—in this case, the HR function—as a business that was providing a return on investment, a very different view from the typical HR model of providing administrative services in response to requests from the operating units, or a cost to be managed.

For Meier, moving into HR was a bit of a leap, certainly not something that she had seen as being on her career path. However, she could see the connection between her skills and what needed to be done in HR, and she could see the vast potential value to be added, so she made that leap.

For many other HR professionals, it was not as clear why HR needed to add this new level of analytical rigor. Individually, they were doing all they could to serve their customers, and the model of HR as a business that "optimized investments" was new to them.

"Trying to explain the application of commercial principles to the function of HR was like learning to speak in a foreign language," Meier says. "I had to learn how to bring the analysis to the table in such a way that people understood what I was talking about."

Meier focused on several areas. One was to reinforce the "right products on the shelf for customer needs" model as a way to rethink HR's approach. She used activity-based costing techniques to put some ballpark numbers around what these products/services cost so that the model was not just a concept and HR staff had numbers to look at. Another was to analyze the metrics they collected with their InfoHRM system to identify five areas to focus on (Figure 10.4).

This model continued HR's evolution toward a function that was much more proactive, actually identifying where the best opportunities for adding value to the business were, not just waiting for the business to ask, or focusing exclusively on process excellence. It was a view that was enthusiastically endorsed by the

Figure 10.4 Major Focus Areas

How we add and measure our value: What the data told us

5 Major Focus Areas	Opportunities	Identified By	
Developing and promoting talent	Ensure optimal talent source	Internal versus total hires, especially at lower levels	
Successful new hires	Maximize investment in new hires	New-hire failure factor	
Ensuring leader's effectiveness	Enhance leadership culture	Leadership effectiveness score, high-potential staffing rate, leader tenure, diversity	Shareholder Value
Managing performance	Improve retention of high performers	Voluntary high-performer termination rate, low-performer termination and turnaround rate	
Optimizing costs	Optimize talent contribution	Talent distribution, brand mix change, span of control, retention risk of critical talent	

CFO, Walter Berman, who felt that there was great value in using metrics to make better HR and people decisions. Ameriprise was moving toward a world where the concept of value creation was embedded in the way all the HR leaders did their work.

Our focus is on the evidence-based change side of Ameriprise's work in HR, but of course other pieces of the puzzle were brought to bear. To complement the infusion of business and analytical thinking that Meier brought to HR, it was important also to have an HR team ready to deliver the HR programs, and processes to drive the outcomes that would be identified. At the same time that Meier joined HR, Hunter also brought in a top HR team with broad talent-management expertise so that when analytics identified opportunities, there was capability to act on them. This is the "process" element of the LAMP model we mentioned in the logic-driven analytics chapter (Chapter One); the step that takes analytical insights and turns them into action.

Multimillion-Dollar Turnover and Other Opportunities

The analysis of the five areas of focus led Ameriprise to tackle three big opportunities.

The first area was turnover, and particularly turnover among high performers and high potentials.

An area such as turnover might not have come to anyone's attention, because Ameriprise turnover levels were comparable to the companies it benchmarked against. Retention levels were high, but when Meier ran the numbers, she could see there was still a substantial opportunity to save money by improving retention of high performers and high potentials. With a staff approaching eight thousand people at the time, there were two thousand high performers, and so improving retention even beyond the current level of 90 percent was a multimillion-dollar opportunity.

Again, this approach to HR was unusual at the time, when the profession was often fascinated with benchmarking and focused on getting HR numbers in line with the appropriate industry average. Yet, from the perspective of a business analyst, things appeared different.

"I didn't care that we looked okay relative to benchmarks," says Meier. "Benchmarks are informational. They don't make decisions for us. There was an attractive opportunity, so we took it."

The analysis led to a series of new high-potential/high-performer programs such as "peer groups" that meet monthly, where members work through various management topics to aid their development. Similarly, there is a leadership program, and a Chairman's Institute that people can be elected to. All these initiatives aim to improve retention among this pivotal segment of the workforce. This approach to segmentation was also unusual at the time because the focus was not simply overall turnover levels and costs but both the impact of turnover among high potentials/high performers and the programs that would most motivate them to stay.

Is there any way of knowing if these programs are working? Yes. The same metrics—high-performer turnover—that led to the initiation of these programs can provide a measure of success. Further measures on engagement, promotion rates, and the average performance rating of people in these programs provide a factual basis to assess effectiveness. If one of these products proves to be ineffective, it will be pulled from the shelf and replaced with something else.

Similarly, an analysis of new-hire failure prompted action. New-hire failure is defined as someone in an exempt job leaving in the first twelve months, or as someone in a nonexempt job leaving in the first six months. Ameriprise was bringing in a lot of people in the wake of the spin-off from American Express—for example, key technical experts, financial reporting experts, and tax experts. New-hire failure is expensive, and Ameriprise saw the value of investing in onboarding to improve the success rate.

HR launched a cross-organization study of onboarding, collected best practices, and then implemented those across the company. One practice introduced was to provide every new hire with a "navigator" who could help them find their way in the complex matrixed organization. They also introduced a "Getting to Know Ameriprise" series of events for employees in their first year. For areas with a high new-hire failure rate, they studied the profile of new employees who were successful and used that to do a better job of selecting people who would stay. As with retention, HR was able to track the success of the program with the same metrics that initiated it: new-hire failure.

A third major initiative was managing performance. Ameriprise is not the sort of place where a poor rating means you are immediately on the way out. There is an attempt to understand the reasons for the poor performance and put in place a plan to improve. So HR added a new metric—persistent poor performance. When persistently poor performers were identified, a performance-improvement plan was put in place, and its effectiveness was closely monitored.

In all these three cases HR at Ameriprise operated in a way quite different from how it had done so in the past. They gathered data, did analysis, focused attention on the areas of greatest opportunity, responded with programs, and measured their success. They were running HR like a business. HR had a conversation with Berman at the time, and he pointed out that driving down high-performer turnover or early-career turnover was a significant opportunity for HR to make a financial contribution.

Beyond Justifying HR

Like all staff groups at Ameriprise, HR is under constant scrutiny as an expense center. However, with this new approach they were easily able to demonstrate that their budgets were justified and that they were adding value. When finance posed the question "Do you really need this budget?" they had the numbers to prove they did. They knew the resources they needed to do a certain amount of hiring, so as long as that amount of hiring was in the plan, they would need those resources. Similarly, based on historical trends, HR knew how many reorganizations to expect, and hence what resources would be required. When the business needs change, HR will change the resources they ask for.

This approach also engendered support from the businesses, where leaders were seeing HR in a new light and were more conscious of the value they added. In the past, HR would typically ask business leaders, "How many new hires will you need?" and then focus on delivering those requests with high quality at the lowest possible cost. But now, as Hunter puts it, "we ask them to think about their sourcing and organizational churn and help them see the potential value in the connections to sourcing and retention in a new way." HR helps them think through issues like retention, sourcing, and development to see the root cause of their business challenges. Finance was delighted by how much discipline HR had instilled around the products-and-services model. Rather than basing the HR budget on such benchmarks as HR staff per FTE, cost per hire, and HR budget to total expense, Ameriprise HR now budgets based on business needs and the products/services HR provides to add value.

Hunter notes, "In our 2011 planning process, we worked through five human capital imperatives to focus on to achieve plan [sourcing, engagement, retention, and so on], and they said, 'Wow, this really makes sense.' They think of us now like their lead financial officer at the table. We went from order takers or program sellers to key business contributors."

Looking to the Future

As HR looks to the future they have a number of areas where they hope to bring a more analytical approach to bear.

"What will differentiate us," Hunter says, "is having ordinary people doing extraordinary things every day. We will get that by continuing on this path of having a smarter and more capable HR function."

Culture, emotions, and values may seem "soft" at first, but the Ameriprise leadership knows that such soft elements are often the key to extraordinary results. The HR team is committed to approaching these things with the same rigorous and analytical approach that has been successful in the past.

While we have concentrated on describing the analytical role HR has been playing, a big part of the function still revolves around the more traditional need to respond to demand from the business. In the future, Ameriprise will be more deliberate about separating what might be called good demand from bad demand. If someone suggests he or she would like to do a reorganization and wants HR support for that, HR is now is a position to provide more discipline in analyzing what the business wants to achieve and whether the proposed reorganization really makes sense.

Another big step for HR will be identifying and planning at a strategic level, around pivotal roles. Pivotal roles are those where an investment in those roles will have a big impact on the execution of strategy. Unlike important jobs, which jobs are pivotal may change from year to year, so Ameriprise will develop processes to regularly refresh the analysis in order to know what the pivotal jobs are in the current situation. This attention to pivotal roles is essential for the leadership team to create an effective strategic workforce plan.

A third new area is to look at the workforce in a more segmented way. They already have special programs aimed at high performers and high potentials, but Ameriprise is thinking about whether it would be useful to look at what they are offering people in their first three years or whatever segments prove to make sense.

The Ameriprise story is not so much about HR activities but about how the company conducts the business of HR through the same lenses that apply to other strategic functions. The message for the reader is not a set of new HR activities or tools, but the consistent principles of using the logic of the businesses, balancing customer needs and ROI, and persistent attention to where the biggest impact will be.

In HR, there can be a tempting gravitational pull toward things like "doing the next new thing to show innovation," "delivering our standard activities as efficiently as possible," or "answering the day-to-day crises and assuming that we are adding value somewhere." These are well-meaning guideposts, but can be misleading. The key is to integrate them with the logic of strategic functions, ROI, and customers' needs.

Managers will encounter moments where they ask, "Does it make sense to be trying this in HR?" That is where you see the power of the principles in this book. It is the ability to have the metrics, target the right issues, act on them, and measure the effect that provides the basis for evidence-based change.

Evidence-Based Change at Ameriprise Financial: Lessons Learned

Sometimes change is sought out, and sometimes it is thrust upon you. In the case of Ameriprise Financial, the rapid spin-off from American Express forced change, but that is not the important story. What matters is how HR embraced using evidence (that is, data and careful logic) to transform the HR function. HR has gone from providing a sprawling collection of services to being a streamlined operation that has a clear and evidence-based sense of how HR adds value to the organization, with the courage to invest and disinvest where it makes sense.

Principle	Lessons
Logic-Driven Analytics	Kano analysis is a sophisticated way in which marketing departments look at the payoffs of enhancing different product features. Taken at its simplest level, it divides product features into *musts*, *wants*, and *delights*. This logical framework helped Ameriprise think rationally about what HR should be delivering and to what level of service. Even without number crunching, the Kano model can bring clarity to where HR should invest its resources.
	The analysis of the costs of turnover among high potentials, even though the turnover rate was not unusually high, is a good example of logic-driven analytics, and it got HR focusing its efforts in an area with a high payback. It also helped transform the businesses' view of HR from a provider of services to a group that helped them leverage human capital based on solid analysis.
	The work on new-hire failure was a similar case of logic-driven analytics driving HR decision making in a way that focused their work on programs that had the biggest financial impact.

(Continued)

Principle	Lessons
Segmentation	We saw a nice example of segmentation when Ameriprise looked at turnover numbers. Rather than just look at across-the-board numbers, Ameriprise segmented out the critical area of high-performer turnover.
	Also in the turnover analysis, they identified the segment where the problem was greatest— early-stage turnover (new-hire failure). This analysis allowed the company to then target an intervention where it would make the biggest difference rather than just trying to improve retention overall by changing rewards or working conditions.
Risk Leverage	Ameriprise did not engage in the detailed risk analysis we saw in the PNC case, but did show a consistent willingness to take risks where there was the opportunity of a big payoff, even when the easier option would have been to avoid the risk. At the broadest level, they chose to reinvent HR even as they were under immense pressure simply to get the basics right. A more specific example was taking a chance on bringing in someone with a finance background rather than an experienced HR person. Both risks have paid off.
Optimization	It is natural for HR to initiate a program on the basis that it does something good or was requested by the business. This approach can deliver reasonable results, but not optimal ones. The products-and-services metaphor Ameriprise adopted encouraged HR to look at all their programs, see how they created business value, and then focus on the best ones. A key part of optimization is the willingness to retire or scale back products/services that, while good, are not the best use of resources. Ameriprise showed courage in engaging in optimization.

11

ROYAL BANK OF SCOTLAND PROVES PEOPLE MATTER

How would you like to be in the middle of your global employee survey process just as your organization came under some of the most intense criticism in decades during a severe economic crisis? In 2008, when financial markets around the world were in free fall, the Royal Bank of Scotland (RBS) Group found itself in just that situation. Many organizations might have canceled or postponed the survey until things improved, but the RBS HR organization saw it as a unique opportunity to test the value of their HR work in the toughest of times. When the crisis hit, they were in the midst of an employee opinion survey and as a result were well placed to assess the impact of the crisis on their employees.

RBS, an organization we have already met briefly in Chapter Five, has often been praised for its advanced HR practices. But it's easy to look good when business is going well. How would HR be judged at a time when the bank was suffering big losses? Before we look at the days of this crisis, it's useful to take a look at what preceded it.

A History of HR Excellence

Janey Smith, HR Director of Organizational Effectiveness, said, "Over the years we have invested in building a strong HR function that is able to create real value for the businesses we support. One area where we have really distinguished ourselves is in our analytical capabilities. We're in the finance industry and our leaders are at home with numbers, so it makes sense that our HR department is, too."

The employee research and insights capability of HR is part of organizational effectiveness, under the purview of a department called Human Capital Strategy headed by Greig Aitken. A banker by trade with an MBA in financial management, Aitken moved into HR in the early 1990s and brought with him an interest in data-driven analytics. Over the next decade, Aitken worked to build up the four main pillars of RBS's Human Capital Strategy:

1. Listening to employees
2. Research capability
3. Human Capital Online
4. Partnership with business leaders

Together these create an infrastructure that allows an effective evidence-based approach to HR, an approach where HR can demonstrate real business impact in good times and bad.

Listening to Employees

The starting point for RBS is to get good data, and one of the potentially most useful sources of data is an employee survey. To go from potentially useful to genuinely useful, the infrastructure needs to be in place to gather not just information but the right information, and then you need to have the resources to analyze it in a way that makes sense to managers.

One challenge global organizations face is that different units do their own surveys, and the organization ends up with fragmented data of limited value. RBS swept away this problem early on by creating a centralized approach to employee surveys. In 2000 it was one of the first to do a global engagement study. Today, there is a single global survey for RBS that is consistent across forty-nine countries, more than thirty brands, and 157,000 staff. At this scale, they could afford to invest substantial effort into ensuring they were asking the right questions in the right way, and selecting questions that would allow them to compare themselves to the other organizations their managers cared about. Their goal has always been to get beyond where leaders would look at a report, say how interesting it was, then put it in a drawer. To achieve that goal took consistent investment in the process over many years.

"You can get a taste for how powerful this is," says Aitken, "when you consider that we have asked every person who is managed by someone how effective that manager is."

By the time the financial crisis thundered along, in 2008, RBS had eight years of experience working with a consistent global employee survey. There is no substitute for simply going through many cycles of the employee listening process so that there is real historical data to provide context, and so that managers have enough experience with the information to know how to act on it.

Getting good data is one thing, but surveys generate so much data that it can be hard to make sense of the results. One technique RBS uses to summarize the results in a meaningful way is with key indices such as:

- Employee engagement
- Leadership effectiveness
- Talent effectiveness
- Risk effectiveness

The first two concepts will be familiar to most readers. Talent effectiveness identifies whether, from the employees' perspective, RBS effectively manages talent across the organization based on questions like "Do you see the right people being promoted?" Too often organizations spend a lot of effort filling in the boxes of a succession planning form, but the real test is whether when a position does become available the person in the "ready now" box is indeed promoted. The talent effectiveness index helps the business know if their talent processes go beyond looking good on paper.

Risk effectiveness is a concept particularly important in financial services and provides insight on the actual effectiveness of risk policies globally. The index rolls up responses from statements such as "I believe risk policies are effective in my business" and "I believe I could report unethical practices without fear of reprisal."

Data are segmented in the usual ways around geography and function, but the more interesting segmentation has to do with zooming in on groups where managers should take action. For example, RBS splits engagement results into four categories; the bookends are those who are highly engaged and highly disengaged. Most of the management focus is on the middle two categories, which they call *striving, may leave* and *not striving, may stay*. The *striving, may leave* segment are staff who are highly engaged but are not committed to staying with the organization. For the CEO of a business, this ought to be of real concern. This is a good example of not just gathering data but presenting it in a meaningful way.

Another segment of interest was contact center staff that left the bank after seven to twelve months. In some places, this short-term-tenure group was in excess of 65 percent of all hires, and simply pointing this out to management was enough to drive changes that got the size of this group down to 15 percent. Aitken says, "Shining the light on the right measure is what makes the difference."

The "employee listening" pillar extends to qualitative information. For example, the global employee opinion survey includes free-text questions that can be analyzed and themed to provide additional insights to support informed business decisions. In 2010, more than fifty-five thousand staff contributed free-text comments that proved invaluable to business leaders as they framed their future people strategy.

In addition, a recent study looked at the effectiveness of the internal functions (such as finance, property, risk, technology, and HR) in meeting the needs of the business. In addition to the quantitative questions, the study included a free-text field: "What are the things this function could do to be more effective and deliver better customer service?" This gave very useful qualitative information from business leaders to the functional heads on how their functions could be improved.

This use of qualitative feedback is not purely confined to employee surveys within RBS. When the CEO, Stephen Hester, issues online communications to all staff across the globe, he includes a place for people to have an online discussion, and this provides an additional rich source of data for the HR and communications groups to analyze for themes or issues to be addressed. Employees have the option to be anonymous, but most do put their names, and the vast majority of the comments are constructive, not just people carping. RBS's embrace of qualitative data is a reminder that no matter how enamored we may be with the analytical power that comes from numbers, evidence-based HR is concerned with all the evidence, not just those things that can be easily counted.

Research Capability

Normally, research projects fall into the hands of individual HR professionals or are passed on to external consultants. However, RBS felt that to truly embed an evidence-based approach into the organization, they needed to build an internal research capability. The internal team partners extensively with external consultants, thought leaders, and academics, but at the end of a project the knowledge remains in-house rather than residing with external experts.

We mentioned the leadership effectiveness index used in employee listening. This index was the outcome of a project the research group did in partnership with the Harvard Business School and a global research team from Towers Watson. They studied how companies that measure leadership effectiveness went about doing it and used that to frame an RBS leadership index. In the best research fashion they took time to test the index worldwide so they could be confident they had a measure the group could rely on to understand the effectiveness and impact of leadership on business performance.

However, perhaps the most important work the research team did was to clarify the causal connections between people data and business data. Historically, some business leaders were not interested in scores on engagement or leadership because they did not see how that information could be translated into something tangible for their business. The research team looked at the relationship between engagement data, sales data, and customer service data. The relationship made it clear to business leaders how effectiveness of people in the branch network had a meaningful impact on customer service. The researchers were also able to show a very strong link between the people measures of leadership and engagement and the business measures of sales and customer service. In effect, they laid out for business leaders the levers they have to enable good business results.

Aitken explained how this can play out in a conversation with a manager. "I might explain that there are areas in your business that have got an engagement index of 84 percent, and another with an engagement index of 11 percent. More interesting, though, in the areas where engagement is low, the customer focus score is 45 percent, compared to 97 percent where engagement is high. Having people with poor customer focus serving customers is going to have a substantial, tangible impact on your business's ability to generate income." This is clearly a much more insightful conversation than just telling a business leader, "This is your engagement index." The research capability makes the employee listening work more effective by explicating the logic that links survey measures to outcomes leaders care about.

Human Capital Online

The third element of the strategy looks inward to building the capability of the HR function. Smaller organizations might envy the HR resources a large organization has, but those resources are not useful unless there is some synergy across the function. If an HR leader in Kazakhstan has to develop a maternity policy on his own, then the fact that he is part of a large global HR department may be moot.

RBS invested in an online global knowledge system for about two thousand HR staff that allows for the latest insights, research, and best practices to be shared efficiently across the group. The lonely HR professional in Kazakhstan can quickly access a wealth of information on Human Capital Online to answer questions across a wide range of topics or submit more complex requests to external researchers, who will provide an answer within ten business days. The sort of information available includes:

- Presentations on employee opinion survey results
- Results of any HR research RBS has done anywhere in the world
- Best-practice case studies HR leaders want to share
- Country guides showing employment conditions, economic conditions, and so on

This is not a hugely complex or expensive system. It took a team of three people six weeks to build the system, and it is kept up-to-date by a small central team.

Partnership with Business Leaders

While HR is responsible for leading employee listening and research, what really makes it meaningful is that they have won support from business leaders. They do this in part by continually thinking not just about HR issues like engagement but about business outcomes like sales and customer satisfaction. A good deal of the communication about the results of employee listening comes directly from Hester, the CEO. That sends a message to staff that RBS takes the information gathered from employees seriously. Perhaps an even more significant indication of how much the CEO has bought in to the value of HR measures is that he has them included as part of his own performance evaluation.

HR puts a great deal of effort into building the partnership with business leaders by preparing the data in a way that helps them take action.

"The challenge for me is that the data we present need to be tangible enough to effect change," Aitken explains. "You cannot just do a presentation of fifty-five slides, because the business leaders will look at it and say, 'What do I do?' Anyone can provide the business with a spreadsheet the length of my arm. What is really difficult is to give a one-page document that tells what the data mean and how to apply them to the business. It's that one-page document, with insights rather than masses of data, that HR strives to provide."

HR is teaching leaders how to think about the business in a new way, to show them the critical cause-and-effect relationships and demonstrate what they can do to improve people management to reach their objectives. It is not just that HR has a good meeting and leaves behind some numbers. HR leaves behind a way of thinking that will guide the managers' actions day to day.

HR also invests time in understanding the business. If you look at marketing or sales reports they can be hundreds of pages long. HR spends time with business leaders to understand which metrics are most relevant. They look for where they think HR insight will help the business move the needle on something significant.

An indication of the success of HR's goal to partner with the business is that Aitken is invited to meet with the boards of each of the fourteen operating units in the RBS group at least once a year. For example, he might meet with the RBS

Americas group to walk through the global opinion surveys, including leadership, engagement, and other "people" measures, and discuss actions that each business will take to effect change.

There is a mutually reinforcing cycle here. If HR produces insights of value to the business, then leadership is more likely to take them seriously. And as the leadership takes HR more seriously, they then invite HR to provide deeper and more frequent insights, and it helps them cement the link from HR insight into business action.

Living Through the Crisis

When the financial crisis hit, HR was in the midst of an employee survey and could see day by day how employee attitudes were affected by events like the collapse of Lehman Brothers. It was disconcerting, but compare it to the alternative. Without data people would walk around the corporate offices in Edinburgh, Scotland, saying, "Employees will be in a panic" or "It's not nearly as bad as it looks" or "No one will care about the training courses now—they'll just be worried about their jobs." There would be no shortage of rumor and opinion, but nothing solid on which to make decisions.

One measure that clearly was suffering was pride in the bank. Before the crisis RBS was lauded in the press, but when some financial companies started to fail, the whole industry was painted as a villain. On the other hand, what people valued did not change dramatically. Yes, employees valued job security, but surveys showed they placed a great deal of value in developmental opportunities as well.

Within HR there was unease, perhaps comparable to that of a musician about to audition for a major orchestra. The team had worked hard and been told they were doing the right things, but this was the test where they would find out if they were any good after all.

Smith said, "We really wanted to believe all the good engagement work the bank had done was real and that there genuinely was cause and effect between engagement and results. As we went through the crisis, we eventually were able to conclude that we weren't getting false positives about our people because of the way we were able to weather the storm."

After the worst of the crisis had passed, RBS looked again at employee survey results and found they outperformed the financial services norm in twelve of the thirteen areas. RBS's financial capital suffered from the turmoil in the industry, but its human capital remained solid, and this set the stage to rebuild profitability.

Rebuilding Pride

The data showed one issue the bank urgently needed to address—pride in the organization. One thing HR picked up on in the surveys was that campaigns aimed at customers actually had a positive impact on employee pride. For example, one way marketing was reengaging customers in the retail operations was to position RBS as the most "helpful" bank. The survey data showed that employees felt very positive about that message. Strong, public, and measurable commitments to customers in marketing campaigns were supporting HR's goal of rebuilding pride.

Another tactic for rebuilding pride was to regularly cascade information about the progress the bank was making on its strategic plans. The evidence that the bank had a clear direction and was doing what it said it was going to do enhanced employees' confidence in the organization.

Knowing what to target and knowing what was working made HR's job in patching weak areas in employee attitudes much easier.

Rethinking Leadership

The shock of the financial crash also shook faith in leadership. If HR really had developed great leaders, why had the bank run into difficulty? The company had seen a massive change in its fortunes, and the burden of responding to that fell on its leaders. HR's task was to support those leaders.

The place to start was strategy. The whole organization's strategy had been repositioned, and RBS decided the most critical step was to make sure every leader understood what was required of them to achieve this new strategic plan. They identified five areas where every leader needed to play a part:

1. *Strategic progress.* Leaders need to create a clear vision for their part of the business based on current and longer-term strategic priorities.

2. *Customer expectations.* Leaders need to put customers at the heart of everything the business does. This means that the needs of our customers are central to the way teams work, that our customers' needs drive the business decisions we take, and that we constantly seek to improve the customer proposition we offer.

3. *Business delivery and financial performance.* Leaders need to deliver sustainable business results to set the foundation for continued growth.

4. *Risk management.* Leaders need to be able to create a culture of transparency and responsible risk management.

5. *People management.* Leaders need to empower, inspire, and motivate their people to give their best every day.

Smith recognized that these demands on leaders meant HR needed to take another look at their leadership competencies. They had an extremely detailed traditional framework of competencies that ran to over fourteen pages. It had been built based on a study of the best leaders, but done back in the days before RBS had become a truly global organization. HR started afresh and distilled the competency model to one page that clearly showed leaders what was expected of them at RBS. This was designed by considering a wide range of diagnostic information including external research around the characteristics of top leaders in successful organizations, and internal analysis of what the employee opinion survey results indicated employees were looking for in leaders.

Validation of the new competency model came from an analysis of about four hundred leadership appointments made in the twelve to eighteen months following the crisis. They used the selection and assessment data of these new leaders to understand subtle but important shifts in leadership success factors. As part of this research, HR put the competency model to one side and just asked leaders to describe what they thought new recruits needed to do to succeed. One important shift in tone in the leadership model was that leaders should enable the potential of their people as opposed to leaders "directing" their people. A competency that might have talked about driving for results shifted in tone to empower, inspire, and motivate people to give their best every day.

To help leaders with these newly framed success factors, RBS reworked their leadership development programs. The old style of leadership development tended to be based on mandatory courses built around case studies. Rather than simply build a new program based on the new competency framework, Smith went out to talk to senior executives to learn what sort of development would be most useful given the new strategic imperatives. Doing this research definitely cut into the time available to design a new program, but they felt the trade-off was worth it. Given how much the banking world had changed, ensuring the training intervention would be relevant to the current needs was more important than having a finely tuned program design.

"In some organizations," Smith says, "the human capital team might sit separately from the leadership development team, which means the leadership development team would be more inclined to just go off and do their own thing. At RBS, because I've got all of these functions as part of my team, we are really able to join up the thinking, and that added more value to the business."

The human capital team in HR worked with the leadership development people to embed measures into the employee opinion surveys so that it was possible to track the progress of all these initiatives. For example, they learned that 82 percent of the global executives found that the performance-management system was extremely effective in helping them deliver their part in developing the strategic plan. Next, they will test the effectiveness of the leadership development program by seeing if the data show any difference between the people who have done the leadership development program and the people who have not. The net effect of these initiatives has been to improve leadership effectiveness.

Past and Future

You don't get great HR simply by spending a year or two implementing some new system. RBS has had a long history of building HR capability and nearly ten years of gathering useful employee data. Over that time, they have learned to dig deep into the data to create useful indices, find causal connections, and deliver meaningful insights. Leaders have learned to trust the data and recognize its importance in helping them achieve business results. Employees have learned their input about the company matters to leaders and that the findings of the opinion survey are acted on. And as RBS moves ahead they can be more subtle in how they use the survey.

"For a number of years, we had quite a regimented process of demanding to see action planning in response to the employee opinion surveys," says Smith. "Now we are more relaxed in letting leaders follow up on the survey the way they see fit, and working with their people to make improvements. That is more important than knowing that by a certain day everyone has reviewed the results and everybody has an action plan. We don't have to be the survey police anymore."

The lesson from RBS is that the investments made in the organization's HR capability before the financial crisis helped see them through that. Post crisis they had a solid footing from which to fine-tune and redirect HR practices to fit the new business strategy. We can expect many interesting initiatives from this group in the years ahead.

Evidence-Based Change at RBS: Lessons Learned

RBS offers one of the best examples of a commitment to evidence-based change. By persisting with its employee survey, even during an unprecedented industry crisis that was certain to have a massive negative impact on employee attitudes, RBS illustrates a key point: evidence-based change is most powerful when the evidence includes both the upside and the downside. By demonstrating the courage to continue to seek employee input even in a downturn, RBS laid the groundwork for later engagement with leaders. The data collected during the downturn allowed rigorous comparisons to similar data before and after. The insights about where employee attitudes changed—and where they did not change—uncovered opportunities to focus change efforts where they were most effective, such as in helping leaders raise the leadership effectiveness index and restoring pride throughout the organization.

Taken in total, the RBS case demonstrates an even more pervasive and subtle example of evidence-based change. RBS leaders now use HR insights as a natural part of their planning and decision making, and use these data-driven people insights to create value for their respective parts of the organization. What began as an HR initiative to uncover and demonstrate the power of HR analytics to business leaders has created a change in the very approach leaders take to their businesses, and their fundamental understanding about the role of talent and human capital.

Principle	Lessons
Logic-Driven Analytics	RBS offers an example of one of the most highly developed HR analytics groups in the world. Many organizations have been reluctant to invest so deeply and significantly in HR analytics, but the lesson of this case is not so much that effective analytics requires a dedicated analytics function. The key is what was done with these resources. The RBS HR analytics group has been able to develop and nurture expertise in advanced analytical methods, creating an in-house capability to unearth relationships in the data that might elude those with less analytical savvy. The HR analytics group has the courage to commit to a centralized management of the employee survey process—allowing units to customize but not to throw out the essential core—because they understand the statistical power of comprehensive data, large samples, and the ability to benchmark. This is the technical excellence side of the story. However, equally striking is RBS's commitment to embedding and framing its HR analytics in logical models and processes that leaders and employees already understand. For example, the case for a centralized and comprehensive employee survey is often made with HR as the "data police," insisting that units complete surveys in the face of apathy or resistance. Here, the case is framed in terms of "every person that is managed by someone gets the chance to tell us how effective his or her manager is." The shift is palatable, and reframes an issue of data completeness into an understandable practical advantage. RBS is in the finance industry, where analytical capability and numbers are key, so it makes sense to apply that same rigor to human capital. That analogy might be made by many business leaders, but making it real is a subtle process of combining the right logic with the right level of analytics. It requires giving non-HR leaders such things as a one-page document summarizing key relationships (rather than massive spreadsheets or slide decks), focusing in on cause-and-effect relationships (rather than presenting disjointed findings and hoping leaders can make some connections), and working hard to find out what outcomes matter most to business leaders *before* doing the analysis. These all combine to produce analytics that naturally appeal and make sense. It is this

(*Continued*)

attention to logic that creates a virtuous cycle where leaders understand the relevance of HR analytics, use those analytics more fundamentally to drive their decisions, and then demand to work with HR to enhance and improve their sophistication.

The logic of connecting frontline employee attitudes to customer attitudes was carried through to create new indices of customer satisfaction for internal functions that don't directly serve RBS's customers but are vital to enabling those that do.

Segmentation

Segmentation and optimization work together at RBS, as illustrated in how the organization parses employee groups on two dimensions—*striving/not striving* and *may leave/may stay*. The consequences of turnover are much higher among the "striving" group, and the risk of turnover is higher in the "may leave" group. The alternative would be an overall engagement ("striving") score, and an overall "likelihood of leaving" score, but the key is putting them together to reveal useful segments. Understanding these segment differences allows leaders to devote their efforts properly and where they have the largest payoff, which is optimization (see "Optimization").

Risk Leverage

In other parts of this book, we showcase risk leverage in terms of the risks that the organization faces or chooses when it comes to human capital, such as mitigating or embracing risks of turnover, stretch assignments, and so on. In the financial industry, attention to risk leverage has been a fixation since the financial crisis, and financial service providers must find innovative ways to insure proper risk taking and risk avoidance. At RBS, we see an example of HR taking this mandate directly and joining it up with the capability to do deep data gathering and analytics. Why not ask employees to comment on a "risk index" with respect to whether they observe leaders taking acceptable risks, feel secure in reporting wrongdoing, and understand and see the effectiveness of risk policies?

In the array of technical measures of risk effectiveness for organizations (which may include complex financial formulas, audits, and legal reviews), the RBS approach reflects the logic that the employees themselves might have insights long before problems emerge. It is instructive that the index focuses not just on whether risks are avoided but on whether they are taken appropriately, which is the essence of risk leverage versus risk mitigation.

Principle	Lessons
Integration and Synergy	RBS illustrates how a data system can motivate synergy across global units, the discovery and sharing of best practices, and integration between the roles of business partners and the global knowledge centers of expertise. Because RBS included a global knowledge system through which business partners can pose their questions to RBS experts, other RBS HR leaders, and outside thought-leading organizations, the best knowledge is integrated and brought to bear where it is most needed. Country guides need no longer be invented from scratch every time a business unit enters a new country but can be leveraged from what has been learned by those that researched other countries. Questions about benefits such as maternity policies no longer rely solely on the expertise of one center of expertise (such as Policy and Employment) or the inventiveness of the HR business partner faced with the question. Instead, by utilizing the global knowledge system such questions can be answered efficiently and effectively. Integration and synergy are also reflected in RBS's skill in using another business analogy: the organizational strategy and competitive positioning rest on the idea of a set of "joined up" financial services, delivered to clients in ways that have been rigorously shown to meet their needs. The RBS logo incorporates this "joined up" symbolism vividly:  In the same way, the human capital analytics at RBS are "joined up" so that the various surveys can be connected with other HR data, such as turnover, performance, and leaders' perceptions. The Leadership Index is joined up with the employee engagement data. Even more impressive is joining up the HR data with tangible and hard-nosed business results, right down to the branch level. That joining up reveals just how significantly RBS's business results are correlated with the results of its employee surveys.

This "joined up" idea was essential to maintaining a commitment to employee data and rigor through the downturn, as the survey began to show that employees' engagement not only affected RBS's service and image but also was affected by it. Employees' pride in the organization was bolstered by RBS's decision to pursue the image of the "helpful bank," revealing there is synergy between strong commitments to customers and employee pride in the organization.

Optimization

Leaders who understand that 25 percent of their population are highly engaged but say they may leave can focus their retention efforts on that group, which is where those efforts will make the biggest difference. Optimizing means not just trying to raise overall engagement scores, or to reduce turnover generally, but to reduce turnover where it has the biggest impact (among those who are "striving").

Optimization at RBS meant having the courage (built out of the necessity to rethink everything after the downturn) to take a fourteen-page leadership competency model, built over decades of consistent industry growth, and refine it into a one-page leadership capability framework designed to reflect the new reality. Leadership no longer meant being good at every conceivable leadership trait but being good at those things that would be most pivotal for the coming challenges. How did RBS identify that new reality? In part it was through the comments from employees about what they felt they needed to see in the new leadership. When employees are provided with the information they need to connect to customers, their insights can drive optimal approaches to leadership development.

Conclusion

Reflections on What We've Learned

Many readers will have experienced how HR shifted from being the personnel department, focused on compliance and administration, to being the department of human resources, focused on providing great services in such areas as recruiting, training, and performance management. The thesis of Boudreau and Ramstad (2007) is that the discipline of HR has not reached the end point of its evolution, and that the next, transformative step is for HR to focus more on decisions about human capital and to educate both HR and non-HR leaders to make those decisions with greater logic and analytical rigor. In this book, we have described five specific principles that embody this new rigor, a rigor that will transform HR as we know it into a much more powerful discipline. In addition, the eleven cases and related stories show how successful HR can be when it has evidence—logical frameworks and data—to drive its change efforts.

Evidence-based approaches must result in real change. RBS's surveys led management to focus successfully on rebuilding pride after the financial crisis. Ameriprise's metaphor of a store's selling a finite range of products helped HR retire low-value-added services. IBM's work on building an enterprisewide talent pipeline increased consultant utilization rates. Khazanah's leadership audits convinced a range of organizations to improve their processes.

The principles underlying evidence-based change bring new clarity to decisions about human capital. In Chapter Two, on segmentation, we saw that there is little point in commercial airlines' requiring their pilots to meet the highest military-grade standards but that it does make sense for airlines to invest in flight attendants who exhibit the very highest level of behavior with respect to customer service. At an airline, a manager's gut instinct might be to use an accounting framework and conclude that the right action would be to focus on pilots, the employees with the highest-paid jobs, and spend less time and energy selecting and developing flight attendants. But HR can combat that gut instinct and help the organization make better decisions by applying the model of return on improved performance (ROIP). We saw this thinking at RBS, where HR leaders got managers focused on dealing with the "striving, may leave" segment of employees, the segment where an investment in retention would have the highest return.

All the individual frameworks we saw deployed in the eleven cases are examples of HR's bringing better thinking to human capital issues. There is no inherent need for these frameworks to be derived from other disciplines, but when they can be, they stand a better chance of adoption. Most of these frameworks are simple enough, and of such general applicability, that there is no reason why HR professionals should hesitate to adopt them. The terms *logic-driven analytics, segmentation, risk leverage, integration and synergy,* and *optimization* belong in HR's everyday lexicon.

Reflections on the HR Leaders

When we look back over the cases and the HR leaders behind them, three attributes stand out—courage, business-mindedness, and boundarylessness (that is, the willingness to stretch beyond the customary limits of HR).

Courage

Courage is perhaps the most common of the shared attributes observed among the leaders at the companies described in this book. All the cases and related stories describe situations in which HR leaders pursued evidence-based change when they could have taken an easier path.

Consider RBS's courage in carrying on with its employee survey in the midst of the biggest-ever financial crisis. It would have been tempting to think that the last thing management needed was bad news from employees, or that the data were not relevant in such extraordinary times, but in fact the survey data proved critical in guiding the bank back to success. The results allowed RBS to identify where investments in leadership and the employee value proposition could be optimized, in line with the bank's emerging strategic imperatives.

HR leaders at Deutsche Telekom showed the courage to call attention to an opportunity, even when they were not facing a crisis. They sensed the value of an enterprisewide talent pipeline and approached that challenge in an admirably disciplined way. They worked to convince stakeholders that the use of common job families and the same assessment tools would allow the organization to enhance the mobility of its talent. This was a win not just for the organization as a whole but also for the employees, who gained better information and more options for developing their careers. From the standpoint of *logic-driven analytics*, what impressed us was the rigor and the process discipline that these leaders brought to the talent-management process.

The leaders at CME Group showed courage when their analysis revealed that the talent needed for new growth was in a segment quite different from the organization's existing core jobs. Their use of the principle of *segmentation* logically led them to the uncomfortable position of having to treat different groups differently. HR leaders did not shy away from that challenge, and through good communication and transparency they gained widespread support. The fact that HR was working from a logical implication of business strategy made this work easier, and it revealed the need for urgency even as the business's stock price was reaching record levels.

HR leaders at PNC Bank were admirably courageous in tackling an area unfamiliar to HR—*risk*. These leaders met that challenge by reaching out to partner with their risk-management function, finance, and their businesses. It was a big undertaking, with many unknowns, and the HR leaders systematically put in place the tools and analytics to help decision makers make sense of the risk associated with hundreds of different incentive plans. They followed up with logical frameworks for mitigating risk through good design and governance. We expect that many HR organizations will follow where (and how) PNC has gone with the principle of risk.

Khazanah Nasional boldly encouraged organizations to share their top talent, in service of creating a world-class national cadre of leaders. It would have been easy to recite all the arguments for why cross-division, let alone cross-industry, talent exchanges could never work, but Khazanah did not hesitate to venture onto this brand-new terrain. As a result, Khazanah found dramatic *synergies* in leadership development.

Shanda is another organization that ventured into the unknown by adopting a game-based HR system. It was impossible for Shanda to look outside for best practices because no one had tried this before. Yet Shanda's HR leaders had faith in the idea of letting their understanding of their talent *segments* and of online games logically drive the creation of a highly *integrated* and *synergistic* HR system that perfectly suited their needs.

Employee surveys are commonplace, but the cases of RBC and RBS illustrate an extraordinary depth of survey analysis. Whereas many organizations look only at descriptive statistics (this factor is high, that factor is low) and at comparisons (this unit gets the best scores, this group gets the worst), these banks demonstrate the wonderful opportunities that *logic-driven analytics* presents. One of the main things RBC and RBS have done is to find employee survey measures that matter, measures that are causally related to metrics that their businesses understand and care about. These two banks have also mined their data to embrace an approach to *segmentation* that can best be seen as lively curiosity. RBS identified the segment "striving, may leave" as being of special interest. RBC segmented by source of hire and realized that the elements of the employee value proposition that mattered most varied from group to group. In common with HR leaders at Coca-Cola, leaders at RBC insisted that HR programs be *integrated* in a way that would provide *synergy*. This is hard work. As we saw in connection with the experience at Coca-Cola, it was not just having common frameworks that made the difference—everyone also believed in them and used them. Neither of these HR organizations took the easy route of resting on its laurels. Both had the courage to press forward with the hard work.

RBC and Coca-Cola are both well-established organizations in a somewhat comfortable position; Ameriprise was anything but comfortable when it first spun off from American Express, yet that did not prevent it from also insisting that HR be more than just a collection of great programs. In the case of Ameriprise, leaders brought in business-mindedness and financial expertise to figure out where HR really added value and where it did not. This was by no means the obvious thing to do. Many would have been satisfied with simply getting the basics right in HR, given the dramatic changes occurring in the organization, and would have found no time for pioneering new approaches. Yet Ameriprise persevered and reached an unusual degree of sophistication in linking HR activities to business outcomes.

At IBM, a clear business issue presented itself—the need to improve consultant utilization rates and implement a globally integrated workforce. Here the company showed both vision and courage in looking to get at root causes rather than pursuing the more obvious tactic of pressuring managers and staff into improving utilization. The idea of treating the talent pipeline like a supply-chain pipeline was a start, but the real genius was in finding a language to make it work and transform how staff were deployed across the business.

The courage shown by the HR leaders we interviewed was complemented by their intensity. No one suggested that evidence-based change was easy, but all were committed to driving the HR function forward and continually raising the bar, even if they were already seen by others as thought leaders.

There was also a sense that they had taken charge of their own fates. The obstacles they faced did not discourage them. They had confidence that HR could do great things, and they were committed to making those great things happen. Although in presenting these cases we have not lingered on setbacks, missteps, or frustrations, these HR leaders no doubt had their share of all three. A high intensity of purpose and a willingness to learn from mistakes were big parts of keeping change on track, and a commitment to evidence-based change gave them the aces they needed to win in the end. HR leaders had the logic and the data and the analytics to convince skeptics that what they were doing made sense for their organizations.

Business-Mindedness

In HR magazines, we often read about the "cool" things that HR departments have done, and the cases we have presented in this book also fit that description. Yet we never got the feeling from the leaders we interviewed that doing something new or cool or clever in HR was at the forefront of their minds. They always started with a focus on the business issues.

It is a cliché that HR should be business-minded, and yet it was such a clear feature of these cases that we would be remiss not to mention it. The link to the business never felt forced, as though HR were struggling to find its own relevance. In the case of Coca-Cola, for instance, the HR strategy flowed directly from the business strategy, and a direct connection could be drawn between the one-page 2020 Vision document and HR's approach. At PNC Bank, HR was responding intelligently to the issues arising out of a very large merger. RBC was interesting in its view that HR was a partner to the business rather than being only a service provider. At RBC, the individual lines of business and HR were all partnering on the goal of long-term success for the organization, and on major issues, such as the employee opinion survey and diversity, what HR was doing was intricately linked to business goals.

Evidence-based change is most powerful when HR is changing the things that really matter to the business. A trait common to the HR leaders we spoke with was being so immersed in the business needs that HR initiatives flowed from those needs.

Boundarylessness

Perhaps a natural extension of the business-mindedness of the HR leaders we interviewed was a certain outward-looking aspect that made it natural for them to partner outside their own function.

It is something we saw again and again. Ameriprise brought in financial expertise, IBM brought in supply-chain experts, PNC partnered with risk management, and RBS tapped outside experts at universities. Boundaries at Khazanah were so flexible that they extended beyond any one organization so that HR naturally embraced collaboration with a wide range of private- and public-sector organizations.

Systems thinking seemed to be self-evidently the right approach in these organizations. RBC saw that marketing initiatives, HR initiatives, and work by the economics department were all elements of a system designed to put the customer first. Shanda saw all the parts of HR fitting together seamlessly into a total employee experience.

Perhaps the lesson we should take from all this is that evidence-based change is not exclusively a technical discipline. It takes character and a mind-set that reaches beyond the normal confines of HR. That character, that mind-set, and those principles lead us to an HR function as different from the typical department of human resources as HR is from the personnel department.

Possible First Steps

As the cases in this book show, there are many ways to implement aspects of evidence-based change. Let us suggest a few areas that offer good starting points.

Analysis of the Risk Associated with Incentives

Incentive risk is not a simple area, but it is one where HR has received much support from boards and CEOs. A lot of this work and learning can be done in the back room, where HR can think through the issues and options before venturing out to rock the boat with suggestions for change. This is a perfect arena for HR to partner with the risk-management function and with consultants to improve analytical savvy, and it presents a useful starting point for a broader discussion of risk.

Segmentation to Refine the Employment Brand

Many organizations have already put a good deal of thought into their employment brand and employee value proposition, and so it is no great leap to apply a supply-side segmentation mind-set here. In the case of Shanda, we saw that supply-side segmentation led to the redesign of HR systems to better engage the company's key demographic. Shanda's willingness to invent dramatically new systems was extraordinary. That degree of ambitious change is rarely required, however. Simply taking a closer look at your most important demographic may suggest improvements to your HR practices.

Segmentation Within a Job

Applying segmentation thinking within a job is not too big a project and generally is not overly controversial. ROIP is a powerful idea, and drawing the curves can give fresh insights into a job.

Once stakeholders recognize where the leverage points for improved performance are, a natural next step is to adjust such HR processes as selection, training, goal setting, and rewards to reflect those leverage points.

Integration and Synergy Within HR

HR can work on improving integration within the HR function without the complication of engaging other stakeholders. A good place to start is to identify some of the key touchpoints where different elements of HR interact and may not be working well together. One area where integration commonly is lacking is the hand-off of new employees from recruiting to the ongoing talent-management system. Recruiting knows a lot about the individual who was hired, but often HR has not made the effort to bring that knowledge into the talent-management system and set it before the managers. Doing that is a worthwhile integration project.

Demographic Change in Mature Markets

In Japan, Europe, and the United States, organizations face an aging population. This situation presents a rich opportunity to apply the five principles of evidence-based change to make sense of the wide-ranging implications flowing from this trend. It offers a great chance for HR to break from the traditional approach of throwing a smattering of disconnected projects (such as stand-alone retention plans or one-off succession plans) at the problem.

As we saw in the cases of Khazanah, CME Group, and RBC, a burning platform is not required in order for an organization to embrace evidence-based change. Nevertheless, if there is a moment of particular crisis or urgency, as we saw in the cases of Ameriprise and RBS, HR leaders can use it to push for more extensive use of logic frameworks and analysis.

A Parting Challenge

The first steps just suggested are only a few ideas to inspire readers. There are many places to start that do not require a massive investment or a move into politically treacherous terrain. The key thing is to get started. Ask yourself these questions:

- *Do we have information overload or persuasive analytics?* Do HR data just sit there, or are they sought out by the business? Is HR information used convincingly to drive better decisions? If you lack persuasive analytics, we hope the cases in this book will point the way forward.

- *Where are our pivotal talent segments?* Are you confident that you know where your pivotal segments are? Do you know what investments will attract and engage them? Do you know what aspects of their performance provide the highest return? If you do not know, now is the time to start finding the answers.

- *Is risk just a four-letter word?* Does your HR department have processes for assessing risk? Does HR have the confidence to distinguish between good risks and bad ones? It is reckless to ignore this issue when it is so much on the minds of boards and CEOs. HR can distinguish itself by being proactive in embracing risk leverage.

- *Is our HR portfolio less than the sum of its parts?* If your individual HR programs are good, but the function as a whole feels underpowered, then that is probably a sign that integration and synergy are lacking. Start with understanding what the business needs are, and then redirect efforts within HR to creating integration rather than adding new programs or enhancing existing ones.

- *Are we "spreading peanut butter" or optimizing investments?* Does HR have the courage and the analytical rigor to optimize investments in the workforce? If you worked at an airline, would you invest more in selecting the very best flight attendants, an area where ROIP is high, than in selecting the best pilots, an area where ROIP is low and where the "average" pilot more than suffices? This is not an easy challenge, but when you embark on segmentation and logic-driven analytics, the payoff will come as you seek to optimize the investment.

Take the plunge, embrace evidence-based change, and transform HR.

Appendix

Summary of Lessons Learned

All the cases in this book have shown HR functions eager to seek out good data and apply rigorous thinking—an attitude that is a fundamental element of evidence-based change. More subtle elements are the commitment to create impactful organizational change and to rely on the best existing research and thinking. The cases show a wide range of examples, from the use of straightforward frameworks focusing attention on key issues (Coca-Cola, Chapter Seven) to sophisticated statistical work showing the relationship between business outcomes and HR metrics (the Royal Bank of Canada, Chapter Six). What all these cases have in common is the mind-set that HR adds more value when it brings more rigor and a greater emphasis on strategic change to questions of how the business approaches human capital. The following table brings together many examples of how the five principles were brought to life in the cases we have highlighted.

	Logic-Driven Analytics	Segmentation	Risk Leverage	Integration and Synergy	Optimization
Ameriprise	Kano analysis divided HR products and services into *musts*, *wants*, and *delights* and identified HR drivers of shareholder value as well as HR services linked to particular drivers.	HR segmented out the critical area of high-performer turnover and discovered that the segment where the problem was greatest was early-stage turnover (new-hire failure).	Ameriprise showed a consistent willingness to take risks where there was the opportunity for a big payoff. Leaders chose to reinvent HR and bring in finance expertise even while under pressure simply to get the basics right.		HR looked at all its programs to see how they were creating value and then focused on the best ones. A key element of optimization was the willingness to retire services that, although good, did not make the best use of resources.
Coca-Cola		HR recognized and met the needs of specific pivotal roles—for example, in India, with its CCU-on-Wheels program that targeted traditional retailers, and in China, with its focus on manufacturing and logistics staff. From the		HR partnered with the business to look at internal changes and global trends as the starting point for defining HR requirements. HR looked beyond traditional HR trends to incorporate consumer and marketplace trends. HR leveraged all aspects of the talent life	

| Khazanah Nasional | Khazanah's Orange Book initiative audited the projected leadership gap and the quality of the processes that were meant to close this gap. | supply-side perspective, the focus on women is a great example of segmentation. | cycle to build capability, whether that meant sourcing talent in China, developing retail capability in India, or grooming the next generation of women leaders. | Khazanah encouraged talent risks both within and across organizations. Organizations were willing to take risks by giving up their talent to other organizations, even though that talent might not return, and even though the development experience might not be effective. | Khazanah leveraged multiple companies and governmental agencies to develop a national pool of leadership talent. The participating organizations were able to develop their leadership talent faster than they could have done on their own. | As the system identified gaps, the priority for development exchanges shifted to emphasize movements that would address those particular gaps. Organizations with excess levels of a competency could be encouraged to contribute more staff through the exchange process, in return for the opportunity to use the exchanges to build competencies that were scarce for themselves. |

(Continued)

	Logic-Driven Analytics	Segmentation	Risk Leverage	Integration and Synergy	Optimization
IBM	HR employed a well-understood business metaphor—the supply chain—as the basis for global human capital planning and defined work requirements to create a logical framework that was detailed enough to be useful and simple enough to be maintained.	IBM initiated its global workforce initiative in the segment of its business that offered consulting and other services, where billable hours and utilization rates provided quantitative data for planning, design, and evaluation. This talent supply was particularly responsive to clear information about development opportunities.	IBM created a system that better articulated risk and return. Leaders' understanding of how project demand and supply were related meant that they could see where it made sense to take risks on talent development. Employees were better enabled to assess the risks and returns of decisions about which competencies to pursue.	IBM recognized that integration and synergy are not automatic in large organizations and saw that idle talent in one country might be needed in another. Once a global workforce management system was built, each country was able to benefit from resources elsewhere in the IBM world. An unexpected synergy was better management of contractors.	The global workforce management system optimized the utilization of people, and investment was focused on those areas where the projected demand was high and withdrawn from areas where the projected need was low.

| Royal Bank of Canada (RBC) | HR's Diversity 2.0 project provided funding to engage marketing experts and to apply their analytical methods and data approaches (such as the use of focus groups and segmentation) in a way that blended the marketing and HR approaches to diversity. | RBC took data from employee opinion surveys and segmented the data on two dimensions—the *business unit* (capital markets versus wealth management) and *gender* (women versus men)—and found that the interaction of the business unit differences and the gender differences revealed opportunities for improving the employee value proposition. | The synergy between business and workforce goals was apparent where RBC's employees' interactions with customers were concerned (for example, the workforce had to speak many languages to attract a diverse customer base). RBC integrated its HR programs in such a way that considerable complexity was held within a small HR group and thus was kept from overwhelming the rest of the organization. | Faced with hundreds of opportunities to provide charitable work to enhance the community, RBC made optimal choices to foster the advancement of newcomers, the inclusion of diverse backgrounds from various schools and communities, and pride in the advancement of newly immigrated groups. |

(Continued)

	Logic-Driven Analytics	Segmentation	Risk Leverage	Integration and Synergy	Optimization
Royal Bank of Scotland (RBS)	The HR analytics group unearthed relationships in the employee survey data that might have eluded those with less analytical savvy. Management of the survey was centralized because the group understood the statistical power of comprehensive data.	RBS segmented employee groups on two dimensions—*striving/not striving* and *may leave/may stay*. The consequences of turnover were found to be much higher among the *striving* group, and the risk of turnover was found to be higher in the *may leave* group, which made the *striving/may leave* segment a particular area of focus.	HR asked employees to comment on a "risk index" regarding whether they observed leaders taking acceptable risks, felt secure about reporting wrongdoing, and saw the effectiveness of risk policies. This approach reflected the logic that employees might have insights into particular issues long before problems related to those issues emerged.	Best practices were shared through the global knowledge center. The leadership index was joined to employee engagement data. Even more impressive, HR data were joined with tangible business results, right down to the branch level. Employee pride was bolstered by the "helpful bank" image, and a synergy was revealed between commitment to customers and employee pride.	Understanding that some employees, although highly engaged, had said they might leave, leaders focused their retention efforts on that group, where retention efforts would make the biggest difference.

The group gave non-HR leaders a one-page document (rather than massive spreadsheets or slide decks) summarizing key relationships.

The index focused not just on whether risks were being avoided but also on whether risks were being appropriately taken.

References

Boudreau, John W. *Retooling HR: Using Proven Business Tools to Make Better Decisions About Talent*. Boston: Harvard Business Press, 2010.

Boudreau, John W., and Ramstad, Peter M. *Beyond HR: The New Science of Human Capital*. Boston: Harvard Business School Press, 2007.

Cascio, Wayne F., and Boudreau, John W. *Investing in People: Financial Impact of Human Resource Initiatives*. 2nd ed. Upper Saddle River, N.J.: FT Press, 2010.

Conaty, Bill, and Charan, Ram. *The Talent Masters: Why Smart Leaders Put People Before Numbers*. New York: Crown Business, 2010.

Davenport, Thomas O., and Harding, Stephen D. *Manager Redefined: The Competitive Advantage in the Middle of Your Organization*. San Francisco: Jossey-Bass, 2010.

Gebauer, Julie, and Lowman, Don. *Closing the Engagement Gap: How Great Companies Unlock Employee Potential for Superior Results*. New York: Portfolio, 2008.

Kanai, Toshihiro. Personal interview with authors.

Nedopil, Dr. Christoph, under the supervision of Professors George Kohlrieser of IMD and Francisco Szekely of the University of Texas at Dallas. "Thinking Outside the Box in Talent Development: Inter-Company Employee Exchange" (A and B). IMD-4-0304 and IMD-4-0305, IMD International, March 25, 2010.

Palmisano, Samuel J. "The Globally Integrated Enterprise." *Foreign Affairs*, 85(3), 2006, 127–136.

Slade, L. Allen, Davenport, Thomas O., Roberts, Darryl R., and Shah, Shamir. "How Microsoft Optimized Its Investment in People After the Dot-Com Era." *Journal of Organizational Excellence*, 22(1), 2002, 43–52.

Sutton, Robert I. *Weird Ideas That Work: 11 1/2 Practices for Promoting, Managing, and Sustaining Innovation*. New York: Free Press, 2002.

About the Authors

John Boudreau is professor and research director at the University of Southern California's Marshall School of Business and Center for Effective Organizations. Boudreau has published more than sixty books and articles. His large-scale research studies and focused field research address the future of the global HR profession, HR measurement and analytics, decision-based HR, executive mobility, HR information systems, and organizational staffing and development. His recent books include *Retooling HR: Using Proven Business Tools to Make Better Decisions About Talent; Beyond HR; The New Science of Human Capital*, with Peter M. Ramstad; *Investing in People: Financial Impact of Human Resource Initiatives*, with Wayne F. Cascio, now in its second edition; and *Achieving Excellence in Human Resources Management: An Assessment of Human Resource Functions*, with Edward Lawler III. Boudreau is a strategic advisor to a wide range of organizations, including early-stage companies, global corporations, government and military agencies, and nonprofit organizations. He is also a fellow and foundation trustee of the National Academy of Human Resources. He has served as a member of the board of advisors for the Human Resource Planning Society and WorldatWork. He chaired the advisory board of the California Strategic HR Partnership, a Silicon Valley HR executive consortium, and served as an advisor to the Saratoga Institute, a global source of human capital benchmarking and performance measures. In addition, he has been elected to the executive committees of the Human Resources Division of the Academy of Management and the Society for Industrial and Organizational Psychology. Boudreau earned an undergraduate degree in business at New Mexico State University as well as a master's degree in management and a PhD in industrial relations, both at Purdue University's Krannert School of Management.

Ravin Jesuthasan, a managing director of Towers Watson, is the global practice leader of the firm's talent-management practice, based in the Chicago office. He has extensive experience in the design and implementation of workforce and people systems that align with an organization's strategic drivers and with the creation of shareholder value. He has also led numerous large-scale, global restructuring and transformation engagements for his clients. Jesuthasan has published numerous articles and led several global research efforts on the topics of labor-cost management, performance management, rewards, and talent management. As a recognized thought leader, he has been a featured speaker on these subjects at conferences in North America, Europe, Asia, and Latin America. He has also been featured in and quoted extensively by leading business media, including CNN, the *Wall Street Journal*, *BusinessWeek*, *Newsweek*, CNBC, *Fortune*, *USA Today*, *Human Capital* (China), *Les Echoes* (France), *Valor Económico* (Brazil), and *Business Times* (Malaysia), among others. He has been recognized as one of the top twenty-five most influential consultants in the world by *Consulting Magazine*. Prior to joining Towers Watson seventeen years ago, Jesuthasan was a consultant with the strategy practice of a major management consulting firm. He holds an undergraduate degree in finance (magna cum laude) and an MBA in finance (summa cum laude). He is a Chartered Financial Analyst and a member of WorldatWork, the Human Resource Planning Society, and the CFA Institute.

Index